How to Adult: Money
Your guide to life in the modern world

(Canada Edition)

Victoria Botvinnik, CPA,CA

How to Adult: Money, Your Guide to Life in the Modern World
© 2017 Victoria Botvinnik

First Edition

For information about special discounts available for bulk purchases, sales promotions, fund-raising and educational needs, contact the author at: HTA.author@gmail.com

Visit the author's website at www.HTAbook.com.

ISBN 978-0-9959826-1-1

Introduction

This book is meant to be your one stop shop for financial advice. Everything you need to know about personal finance, savings, debt, taxes, and investing at the non-professional level is in the pages you're about to read. But don't run away screaming just yet, I'll try to make it as painless as possible. I'll even tell you some jokes, but I can't promise they'll be funny. We'll go through a week by week program to help you get your financial life in order. It'll all be fine; we'll get through it together. I've put all the useful spreadsheets on my website for you to follow along with[1].

Young people today are really worried about money. According to some research about millennials conducted in 2014[2], 73% of people in the poll were on the spectrum from 'somewhat worried' to 'very worried' about retirement. Yet, they do nothing (at least nothing constructive) to make themselves less worried. But why should that be the case? You don't need to be afraid of the stock market and investing. Closing your eyes and hoping for the best won't help you, and it definitely won't change your future for the better. Neither will ignoring investing and savings because you're afraid of failing. You know what might? Saving enough money to be okay in retirement. Learning about investing so that your money can work for you instead of sitting in your bank account. Even understanding basic personal finance concepts like credit cards and mortgages will help you have more control over your finances.

That's basically it. I'll teach you what you need to know to be in charge of your money. There won't be any extra stories in this book. I won't tell you my life's story. Nobody cares about that. I want you to get in and get out with mad knowledge and useful new habits.

Let's go!

Table of Contents

Part 1: Personal Finance

Part 2: Budgets and Saving

Part 3: Investing

Part 4: Taxes

Part 5: Six Months to Being Awesome With Money

Part 6: Financial Independence

1 Personal Finance

What is Personal Finance?

Personal finance is everything that's not specifically saving or investing. All the random financial information your parents just seem to inherently know, but don't think you need to learn or don't know how to teach you. These are the basic concepts that everything about investing and savings is built on, with some extras that didn't really belong in the other sections.

Let's start with one of the simpler things that everybody should have, bank accounts.

Bank Accounts

Bank accounts allow you to deposit money and make transactions with it. Your name and Social Insurance Number are used to identify that the bank account is yours. This is where paycheques go and your life's expenses come from. Most people have three types of accounts: Chequing, Savings, and Investment.

Chequing

A chequing account is the place where all of your financial things happen. Your wages will be deposited here and you'll pay your credit cards from here, everything goes through this account. This is the most important account to have, so there are many banks that offer them.

However, you should really shop around for a bank on this one. Some of them tack on annoying fees if you don't have enough transactions that make just having a bank account expensive. Others will ask you to keep a minimum amount of money in an account to avoid those fees. Be wary of these and do some research. There's really no need to pay a bank to do its job, they make money off you in other ways.

If you're a student, you'll likely be able to get a decent account without much research since students are sought-after customers. Try and keep that account once you're no longer a student. The banks don't usually put up a fight. Banks offer these accounts cheaply so they can sell you all of their expensive new products as you grow up and make more money (credit cards, mortgages, etc. We'll talk about these in a bit).

Chequing accounts pay very little interest, so don't keep more money than you need in them. I would recommend keeping two weeks' worth of transactions at most if you're salaried, a month if your income is more precarious. Everything else should go into the next two accounts, depending on your money goals.

Savings

A savings account is a place where you park any cash you need in the short term, say three to five years. Saving for school tuition next year? A down payment for a house or apartment? A big trip? Buying a pet leopard soon? It all goes here.

Interest terms are slightly better here than in chequing accounts, but are still fairly low. Again, keep only the amount of money you actually need in here since it's not really working that hard for you. The most important thing about money is how hard you can make it work for you and earn money on your money.

Savings account fees are fairly low due to the low transaction volume in these accounts (fewer instances of money coming in or going out). Hopefully, you'll make regular deposits that correspond with your pay schedule. Banks don't make much money on these accounts themselves, it's all in the expensive products outlined below. So beware of the promotions they'll try to hook you in with.

Investment

An investment account is the place where long-term money goes. You can buy and sell different types of investments in these accounts and they can be linked with your other accounts or held in a different institution. Provided you actually invest it, your money will multiply in these accounts, just for existing.

These accounts have no interest or fees unless you make a transaction. We'll talk about that in more detail in the investing section of this book.

Additional Information

You can have a shared bank account with other people, generally a parent or a significant other. Unless you're underage, this is a bad idea. Having other people attached to the account allows them to use it as they please and the account will be affected by any bankruptcy or debt that this other person has been involved in.

A weird situation will occur in the event of the death of this person. The account is frozen and becomes a part of their estate. If this is your main bank account, that could cause major issues.

Cheques

Cheques are little pieces of paper that give someone your permission to withdraw a certain amount of your money.

Anatomy of a Cheque

```
Your Name   ①                              ⑧ 0001
Your address                          Date___②_____

Pay to the
order of  _____③_____  $ [  ④  ]
          _____⑤_____  Dollars


Memo____⑥_____        _____⑦_____
  ⑧        ⑨         ⑩       ⑪
 0001   123456789   678   1234567
```

1. Name/Address: Where your name and address goes. If you're sharing an account with someone make sure both names appear here.
2. Date: Standard format is month/day/year, or you could write out the name of the month if you like.
3. Payee: Who are you paying? That person's or company's name goes here.
4. Amount: The amount you're willing to pay for whatever it is the cheque is for. Make sure to write out the cents too!
5. Written Amount: Write the same amount you wrote above on this line, but in words. This helps the bank in ambiguous situations where your writing is illegible or if someone tried to change the number.
6. Memo: Make a little note to yourself for future reference to record what the money was for. 'Rent Oct 2016' or similar. This will help with tracking expenses which we'll discuss later.
7. Signature: A bank will not cash a cheque without a signature. When paying for something with a cheque, you must sign the cheque in order for the receiver to be able to cash or deposit it.

8. Cheque Number: Allows you to keep track of cheques you've written. This is helpful when one is lost or stolen.
9. Transit Number or Branch Number: Refers to the specific branch of the bank that you have the account with. Generally this is the building you walked into to open your account. This lets your bank take the money from the right branch.
10. Financial Institution Number: Tells the bank depositing your cheque what bank you have the account with so they know who to ask for your money. Each bank has its own unique number.
11. Account Number: Which account the bank needs to take the money out of.

Do People Still Use Cheques?

Aren't they ancient history? Depends on who you ask. A good amount of people would rather use their online banking accounts to transfer money electronically to other people, so cheques are mostly dead for that use. Honestly I don't blame them, online banking is the bomb. Unfortunately, they are still heavily favoured by landlords and have some other limited uses. Get at least one book of cheques when you open an account, it'll last you forever. (Some banks will charge for chequebooks though, so keep that in mind.)

Post-Dated Cheques

Speaking of landlords. Post-dated cheques are a promise to pay a certain amount of money in advance. For example, most rental agreements require all 12 months of payments in post-dated cheques at the signing of the lease so they don't have to bother you every month for a new cheque. Each cheque will have the monthly lease date on it, allowing the landlord to cash it only on that date or after, but not before. That's the beauty and usefulness of the post-dated cheque, it allows you to promise someone money at a point in time, but never before that specified date. You can promise money you don't have yet, fun!

Void Cheques

These are generally used when you get a new job and they need to
deposit your earnings directly into the bank, a system called direct
deposit. You've probably heard of it, but in case you haven't, it's a
system where an employer doesn't hand out cheques every pay
period and instead puts the money into your bank account on the
right day. The void cheque is the easiest way for both parties to
make sure the information you give them about the account is
correct. Since a cheque has all the same information they'll need
to put money into your account, that's all they need.

To void a cheque, take a cheque from your cheque book, write
'VOID' on it in huge letters and give it to your new employer so
they can have all the information they need to put money into
your account. The 'VOID' makes sure that the cheque can't be
used to take money out of the account if someone gets their hands
on it. Banks will not cash cheques marked in this way. There are
also direct deposit forms the bank can give you with the same
information if you don't want to waste cheques, they are expensive
after all.

Certified Cheques

You have to go into a branch of your bank for these fancy cheques.
By issuing this type of cheque, the bank confirms that you have
the amount of money in your account at the time of certification.
It gives the recipient of the cheque confidence that the cheque
won't bounce and that your account is genuinely yours. That's why
many people treat certified cheques as if they were cash, because
the money is guaranteed. Sometimes the bank will even set aside
the amount of money that was certified to ensure you don't move
it out before it's cashed. A bank draft is similar to a certified
cheque, except the funds *must* be set aside and will not be
returned back into your account until they are withdrawn by the
recipient or you cancel the draft. Both certified cheques and bank
drafts are generally used when large amounts of money have to
change hands between individual people. You're probably only see
these types of cheques when putting a down payment on a home
or a car.

Credit Cards

What is a Credit Card?

A credit card is a piece of plastic that allows you to spend money you don't have, and doesn't ask you pay it back until a month later. Who doesn't love temporarily free money? Some cards even have cool benefits like airline points or cash back on amounts spent.

The amount you're allowed to spend is called a credit limit and if you don't pay it at that month end point you'll get charged interest on what you owe.

Some specific credit card types are:

Secured Credit Card: Are you new on the scene or recovering from a bad credit score (more on this later)? This type of card might be for you. You'll have to put up cash collateral in order to use this card, and that amount becomes your credit limit. If you put in $5,000, you can charge up to that amount on the card.

Co-signed Credit Card: In this situation, you share your credit card with another person, probably one with a better income or credit score who can vouch for you so that you get approved for the card. You are both on the hook for the spending done on the card, so this is a dangerous thing to do for somebody. Pick your co-signer carefully.

Regular Credit Card: The most common type of card. You get approved for a certain credit limit based on your income and credit score, with no collateral. Some of these cards come with sweet perks like earning airline points, at which point they're called Rewards Cards.

Should You Get a Credit Card?

Hell yes. Credit cards are great as long as you can pay for what you buy and limit yourself to only getting things you can actually afford.

Credit cards are a great way for you to build something called credit history, which then flows into a credit score. Your credit history is your history of taking out loans and paying them back. We'll dive deeper into that in a few pages.

Why is this useful? Because if you want to buy a car or house using a loan (since buying a house with cold hard cash might be hard), whoever is giving you the money to do it will want to know how good you've been with debt in the past and will set the interest rate accordingly. A credit card allows you to show debt management skills without having to take out huge loans you don't need just to prove you're a trustworthy person.

Credit cards are a 30 day interest-free loan. But if you can't pay after those 30 days you're not going to have a fun time.

APRs (Annual Percentage Rate)

If you want to keep their money for longer than 30 days, the APR is the interest rate the credit card company will charge you. It's generally in the 15-20% range, which is ridiculous and why you should really only buy what you can pay for.

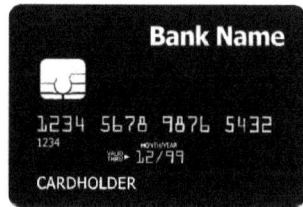

The problem with large interest rates is that they compound. If you bought an expensive TV last month for $4,000, but won't have the money to pay until after your first month at a new job five months from now, you're actually going to be paying quite a bit more for that TV when you pay that debt down. $345 more to be exact, just for the privilege of having the TV a few months earlier.

Carrying a balance on a credit card should be avoided at all costs. It can trick you into paying way more for something you don't even care that much about. Especially if you can't pay them down for an extended period of time, whether it's due to an inability to work or other issues.

Dangers of Credit Cards

Credit cards are a great thing to have if you know how to use them without being used and abused *by* them. One of the most dangerous things about credit cards is the temptation to spend more money than if you were paying cash. One study conducted in 2001 showed that you could potentially spend up to 100% more using credit cards then you would using cash[3]. Using the card is so convenient you don't think as much about your purchases. When paying with cash you would have to literally hand over hard-earned money. Swiping a credit card hurts a lot less. If you decide to use credit cards, you should keep this in mind when you're about to make an impulse purchase.

Another danger is that paying the minimum might make you feel like you're being a responsible adult by dealing with your debts. But, if you're only putting in the minimum payment, you'll cost yourself a ton of interest on the balance as it keeps growing while you chip away small pieces of it. You're not really paying down the debt by much, if at all. Understanding that the entire balance, and not just the minimum payment, is your debt will hopefully help you avoid this pitfall.

It's also pretty easy to forget (or purposefully not read) your statement when it comes every month. This could have two unintended consequences. By not reviewing your spending for the month, you might miss errors or identity theft committed using your card. A more likely, but less extreme, danger is that you won't hold yourself accountable for the purchases you make. Out of sight, out of mind, am I right? This kind of behaviour could derail you pretty hard if it goes on for a long period of time. Check your statements! Not just the total balance.

The fine print on your credit card agreement can also come back to bite you. Did you know many credit cards have a clause that increases the interest rate after a certain number of non-payments? If you forget to pay off a card a few times, your interest rate could skyrocket! Always read the fine print before agreeing to take the credit card because you never know what terms they'll spring on you.

On top of all that, credit cards are positioned as something that helps you live your life. While credit cards are indeed super convenient, credit card companies don't offer them to people out of the goodness of their hearts. Credit cards make VISA, MasterCard, and AMEX a ton of money. VISA alone brought in $15.1 billion in revenue in 2016[4]!

It's their job to keep you in debt and paying interest (and they're really good at it), so don't believe the hype. Use credit cards wisely and pay off your balance in full each month so you can get free monthly loans and rewards without giving the companies anything more than you need to.

Credit Scores

Told you I'd get to it. Your credit score is one of the most important financial numbers in your life. It tells a potential lender whether or not you're trustworthy enough for a loan, and if approved, it determines the terms of the loan (how much interest you'll pay and how long you will have to repay that loan).

Credit scores are required for phone contracts, mortgages, car loans, and leases. Some people and companies will even use your credit score to judge you for non-financial things like whether you're serious relationship material or if you'd make a good employee. I'm not kidding–this really happens!

| 760-850 Excellent |
| 700-759 Very Good |
| 660-699 Good |
| 620-659 Fair |
| <619 Poor |

What Affects a Credit Score?

Credit scores are finicky. They can be influenced by many factors and take some time to improve if you've been naughty with your credit. The basic formula to determine a person's score goes a little like this:

35% Payment History

Consistency and timeliness are what the credit agencies like to see in this category. How many times you've forgotten to pay a credit card bill will affect your credit score in a big way. While the weight of each loan on your score is unknown, some agencies have noted that bigger loans have a bigger influence. Forgetting the mortgage payment will ding your score much harder than forgetting a credit card bill (or maybe the other way around, if you like expensive things).

30% Credit Utilization

Credit utilization is the ratio of credit outstanding (owed) to credit available (your credit card limit). The less money you owe, the better in the eyes of the credit agencies, as long as you have the room to borrow. According to some agencies, people who carry large credit balances are seen as having trouble responsibly managing their debt[5]. For the best credit scores, you should aim for 0-20% utilization. This could mean either having a large credit limit or barely using credit, whichever works for you. Spending $200 with a $500 credit limit (40% utilization) is different from borrowing the same amount on a $5,000 credit limit (4% utilization).

15% Length of Credit History

This piece of the puzzle is why everybody always tells you to 'build credit' in high school or university/college. The longer an account is open, the better your score. A longer history shows a lender a clearer view of your financial behaviour. To keep your score high, avoid closing your oldest credit cards.

10% New Credit

Opening too many credit accounts at the same time can make you look as if you're in dire need of cash. This kind of behaviour worries lenders and makes you seem less trustworthy to them. To keep your score as high as possible, only take on debt or open new lines of credit when you actually need them. Your credit score is temporarily dinged each time it's requested by outside parties, which happens when you apply for loans.

10% Credit Mix

Lenders and agencies prefer to see a variety of credit types in your history. It shows them that you can handle all sorts of debt. However, there's no point in taking on debt you don't need just to have a good credit mix, so this is one of the less important categories.

In general, focus on the first three portions of the calculation: pay debts on time, don't carry a large balance, and have a long history. If you've made a few money mistakes in your past that have led to a bad credit score, it could take six or seven years of good behaviour–the maximum amount of time negative credit related information can stay on your record–to bring it back up.

What are Credit Reports?

Credit reports are official reports about your credit you can get from companies that track credit information. These companies are called credit bureaus. Information on all credit cards and loans that have ever been taken out on your Social Insurance Number will be included on those reports. You can also get a report with your score on it.

Credit reports have two main users, lenders and yourself. Most lenders can get your score if they need it for a phone plan or a mortgage without your direct involvement; they just need your permission. However, it's a good idea to get one yourself once in a while to make sure all the information on your credit report is consistent with your knowledge of what you owe. If anybody has committed identity fraud against you, the credit report will be one of the easiest ways to spot it. Identity fraud can look like loans you never applied for, potentially in places you've never been. Sometimes, parents take out loans in their children's names, so do look out for that as well.

Once a year, you should be able to get your credit report for free from each credit reporting company without it hurting your score. This report does not include your score, but it is still useful for checking your accounts. To get the actual score, you'll either have to get an estimate from your credit card company or pay for a report from one of the companies below.

To get a credit report in Canada you have two options: Equifax and Transunion. Both cost around $25 for an online credit score and report.

Wrong Information and Identity Theft

What happens when you get your credit report, and the information on it is wrong? Or worse, the debts belong to another person who really sucks at paying them?

If you find something inaccurate in the report, it's your responsibility to report it and get it removed. For this very reason, check your report about once a year (it's free anyways).

Pay careful attention to each line item since this is a creditor's only way of assessing your value as a borrower.

Once reported, the credit bureau has to remove any incorrect information within 30 days of being notified. Notify them by using snail mail with a receipt confirmation so that you have proof of notification if the credit bureau is unresponsive. After they receive the letter, the credit bureau will try and sort out the issue with whatever creditor is saying you owe them money. If the credit bureau still thinks their information is correct, you have the right to go directly to the creditor and try to resolve the issue with them. If all else fails, you can add a Consumer Statement to your file. It's a short explanation of the issue with a particular item. If you're still not satisfied with the resolution, you can go higher up the food chain to get it resolved[6].

What if it's more than an error? If you think someone purposefully used your Social Insurance Number and name to open a loan somewhere, that's a whole other story, especially since it's often someone you're close to. The first thing you need to do is call the credit bureau and place a free Fraud Victim Alert on your account. You can also freeze your credit for a small fee with each bureau. The Fraud Victim Alert lets anybody checking your report know that the report is in dispute. It will be difficult for you to get new credit during the time it's in effect though, if that's important to you. Oh yeah, about that criminal activity, filing a police report is the next step. Regardless of who committed the crime against you, family member or stranger, it's still a crime. Make sure to let the police know if you suspect someone you know. If you have a police report filed, the Fraud Victim Alert on your account can be extended indefinitely so everyone involved is aware there's a problem.

The next step is to contact the creditor directly and plead your innocence of the debt. If you have any documentation that could help convince them you didn't spend the money, this would be the place to provide it. Keep bugging them and it will eventually get resolved.

How Many Credit Cards Do You Need?

There are apparently 68.5 million VISA and MasterCard credit cards floating around in Canada[7]. For a country with half that many people, that's pretty crazy. This means that people are holding three, four, or even more credit cards!

Why do people need that many cards? The short answer is they don't, the cards just show up in their mailbox or when they go to the store. How many times have you received credit cards in the mail that you didn't ask for and never applied for? How about being pressured to sign up for a store credit card at check-out? Probably at least a few times. What did you do with those offers? Some people probably just accepted them and those cards sit in their wallets now.

But how many do you really need? As long as you can be responsible with paying both off at the end of the month, I would say two is a good number. You should have one of each of the main credit card companies, VISA and MasterCard. This is so you have a spare if one is lost or stolen. Some stores only accept one or the other, so it's good to have both. I chose those two companies because the other main competitor, American Express, is not as widely accepted.

Rewards Cards

Are cards that give out special rewards worth it? Airline miles, free groceries, and cash back are all very nice to have. The issue with these cards is that many of them charge you an annual fee just to use them. So whether the card is worth it is a simple calculation: how much you expect to spend on the card in the year, how much the fee is, and how much of the reward you could get.

Let me show you two quick examples:

Flight Rewards: A card has an annual fee of $120, a 15,000 point signup bonus, and gives you 1 point per $1 spent. If you spend $30,000 a year on this card, at the end of one year you would have 45,000 points.

This is enough for a round trip to Hawaii! But bear in mind it's only the airfare that's free, you still have to pay taxes on these flights, and they are usually quite expensive due to the airlines with whom the credit card companies are partnered. In our case it's Air Canada which will charge me $179.26 for a return flight in March. The retail amount for a similar flight in the same timeframe is $595. That's savings of $295.74.

$595 retail - $179.26 with points - $120 fee = $175.74 of benefits

Would you spend $30,000 to only save $176? The answer depends on the person and whether you would have spent that money anyway. Remember that it's much easier to spend money on credit!

Cash Back Rewards: A card has an annual fee of $100 and will pay you 2% cash back on groceries and 1% cash back on all other purchases. If you spend the same $30,000 (split 50/50 between groceries and other), you'd have made a cash back total of $350 after the annual fee. Again, whether that is worth it to you really depends on what you spend your money on.

Most of these cards are only worth it if you spend a lot of money on a regular basis and if the fees are low. This is why many people try to route their rent payments through credit cards. There's also a way to get more benefits out of these cards called churning, but it's not without its risks.

Churning

Churning is the practice of applying for multiple credit cards that have good signup bonuses, getting the bonuses, and then closing or downgrading the card as soon as the promotional period is over. This is how many people get free flights and how some of those travel bloggers get to all their amazing destinations without going broke.

This method is a great way to get cheap vacations, but as with anything else, moderation is key. Remember that every time you apply for a new credit card, your credit score will take a small temporary hit. If you open ten credit cards in one year, your credit will be hit ten times, and it's going to be dinged up pretty badly for a short while. Opening and closing multiple credit cards also creates a yo-yo effect in your length of credit history and in the amount of credit utilization you have, since each credit card is added or subtracted from your report, ten times over. Whether the couple of flights that you may have gotten out of those cards were worth it would be a question you'd have to answer yourself. If you don't plan on buying real estate or anything you'd need a big loan for anytime soon (a year or so), then go right ahead. You'll have more than enough time to fix your credit over that time period with saintly credit behaviour.

Keep in mind that credit card companies are getting wise to this practice and might crack down on it soon. Take advantage of it while you can! Many credit card companies will only allow you to have a certain amount of their cards at a time and will remove signup bonuses if they see that you've had the card before.

Pension plans

You're young, why should you care about retirement plans? Because retirement is inevitable. You'll turn old and grey whether you like it or not. Unless you die horribly in a freak accident before you turn 65, but let's not think about that morbid possibility. Given that you'll (most likely) get old, you might as well learn a bit about your options and how they affect a future retirement situation.

A pension plan is a job related benefit an employer is likely to offer you if you're a full-time employee in a big enough company. It's a program that holds your hand through saving for retirement and it's great because it can be a way to get free money. Do I have your attention now? Good.

Defined Benefit Pension Plans

The unicorn of pension plans. They guarantee you $X per month for the rest of your life when you retire. Plans like these mean you have to save very little for retirement because the company will do it for you, and any risk of investments not working out falls squarely on the company's shoulders. They literally owe you money no matter what.

Sounds amazing, how do you get one of these? Most of the time you'll have to work for the government or a very old organization. Those are pretty much the only companies that still offer these babies. On top of that, you'll have to work there for a minimum amount of time to get it, usually 20 years and up. For today's careers of multiple short stints at different employers, this would be hard to do even if you were to find a willing company.

But if you manage to get into it, you'll receive a certain % of your

income at the company for the rest of your life (provided the company doesn't go bankrupt).

The amount you get will be similar to the formula below:

$$(2\%) \times (\text{Years at the company}) \times (\text{Average of your best 5 years of salary})$$

If the average of your best 5 years at the company is $90,000, and you worked at the company for 25 years, you'll get an annual pension of $45,000.

How does this work? Every paycheque the company will take some money from your wages and invest it for you. They will manage the investments so you won't have to see or worry about any of that stuff. When you turn 65 and retire, you'll get payments every month at a predetermined amount for the rest of your life.

Defined Contribution Pension Plan

Companies prefer this type of plan because it makes no promises to employees about what they'll receive in the future, which is why this plan is very common nowadays. Companies want to save money, shocker. These plans are investment products provided by your employer where you may contribute a portion of your paycheque and the company will help you invest the money. The employer may put some money in for your retirement or it might not, but in this scenario, you are solely responsible for retirement saving and investing. The company only provides the account, investing options, and maybe some advice.

Most medium to large sized companies offer these types of plans, so if your employer is not a startup you should have access to one. They're generally not available to contract or part-time workers, so full timers only.

Back to the free money I was talking about earlier. It's called the employer match, and it's what happens when your employer helps you contribute to your retirement. It's generally done in the following way: you promise to contribute a certain percentage of your salary to this plan and your employer will match it up to a point. This is fantastic and you should take advantage of it as soon as you're allowed to. Generally, there's a probation period of some sort.

Most companies will partner with a large financial company and give them control over the investment choices of the plan. We'll talk more about smart retirement investing later on, but all you need to know now is that you should be putting in the minimum amount to get the employer match, at least.

When you leave an employer, these plans can be kept in your name at that same financial company or transferred to a new employer's accounts. It's generally an easy process handled by the financial companies themselves. You can also transfer it to a self-managed account after you've read Part Three and become super good at investing.

Rent or Buy

Where you live is a huge and very personal decision. But before taking the plunge and deciding to buy or rent a place to live, you should keep the financial aspects of it in mind. Ditto for deciding the size of your residence.

Homes come in all sizes and price points depending on where you live. Housing options in a city and those in a rural area are very different. So first, you should decide where you'd like to live for other reasons. These reasons can be anything you like: where you work, where your family lives, where your preferred weather happens, what activities you like to do, if you like being able to walk places, etc.

Once you've decided where you want to live, let's start talking about how you want to live. Do you want a house, an apartment, or something in between? This decision is one you make yourself and the factors that go into it are beyond the scope of this book.

For this exercise, you need to decide the type of home you'll live in. This can be an apartment (condominium or otherwise), a house or its many iterations (townhouses, duplexes, etc.), or a shared living situation (a basement or a room share). This section applies to the apartment or house decision since obviously you can't buy a basement on its own.

Should you rent or buy the type of home you choose? That depends, and there's some math involved. Buying a home is not always the right decision. The old adage about 'throwing money away' by renting may not be true depending on the area you choose to live in and the potential to make money from investments.

HCOL versus LCOL

Yay acronyms! Speaking of places to live, the country is divided into High Cost of Living (HCOL) and Low Cost of Living (LCOL) areas, with some areas in between the two. HCOL areas are generally populated city centres and LCOL areas are less populated cities and rural communities. The general rule of thumb is the higher the cost of living in an area, the less advantageous it is to buy. In general, this is due to high property taxes, high purchase prices, and large availability of rental units. In LCOL areas, all those factors are generally friendlier to those looking to buy.

To get an idea of whether you should rent or buy, you need to plug your particular situation into a calculator that uses all the costs of buying weighted against the costs of renting, with any excess from renting being invested in the stock market. The investing portion is very important. If you don't invest the difference between renting and buying you *will* be throwing money away, since you won't be contributing to an asset that increases in value. When you buy a house, you'll have something to sell at the end of it. With renting you won't unless you stash the difference into investments. We'll discuss investing later, but this is the most important aspect of this decision that people miss.

The Calculation

What are the factors that determine whether it's better for you to rent or buy?

Home Price

The higher the home price, the more money you'll be paying interest on over the life of your mortgage. It also increases the amount you need to save for a reasonable down payment. The higher the price, the more expensive buying becomes compared to renting.

Duration of Stay

The longer you stay in one place the more the tables turn in favour of buying. It reduces the burden of all the costs of buying and selling a home because it spreads them out over a longer period of time.

Mortgage Rate

Mortgage rate is the interest rate you'll be paying on the money you borrowed to buy the home. The higher this is the better it would probably be for you to move money into the stock market, where it will earn money instead. Hence the higher the mortgage rate, the better the deal for renting. As an FYI, the banks don't set the mortgage rates themselves; they build on the interest rates in the general economy which are set by your country's Central Bank.

Real Estate Growth Rate

This measures how much more your home will be worth when you sell it. A high growth rate means you'll be better off buying because you'll get a nice payday (tax free) when you move. The real estate growth rate is not something you can bet on or predict, but it's an important factor to be considered.

Investment Growth Rate

On the opposite side of that coin, the better the growth that you can expect from investments, the better off you'd be renting and pouring your money into the market. But again, this is another unpredictable aspect of the world.

Rent Growth Rate

How much a landlord can increase rent on you is generally written into city or municipal by-laws. You should be knowledgeable about these, since the higher the rent growth rate the less likely it is that renting is the better option. If there is no mandated maximum on rent increases in your area, this is a bad sign for renting. No one wants their rent raised 20% in one year!

Property Tax

Property taxes vary widely across different areas. In some places, they can be a ridiculously high percentage of your home's worth. Generally, these areas are also quite expensive to begin with which exacerbates the problem. The higher the property tax, the more expensive it is to buy since this is an annual cost.

Maintenance Costs

Renovations, condominium fees, homeowners' association fees, utilities, and homeowners' insurance are also costs which need to be considered when owning a home. The more expensive these annual ongoing expenses are, the more expensive it's going to be to own a home.

Those are the main and most influential items to consider when making the buy or rent decision. I'm not going to lay out the mathematical formula for this decision here because it's long and ugly. Instead, here's[8] a very popular calculator that will tell you what rent amount would be comparable to the costs of purchasing the type of home you're looking at.

For a quick example, let's say you want to live in a one bedroom condominium apartment in a large city. Apartments cost $350,000 or rent out for $1,800, which is the better deal? We'll make the following assumptions which you can play with in the calculator, all for a 9 year living period.

- 20% down payment
- 4% mortgage interest rate
- 30 year mortgage
- 3% annual home value growth
- 1.5% property tax
- 4% cost of buying home (legal, inspections, etc.)
- 6% cost of selling home (staging, legal, commission to real estate agent, etc.)
- 1% annual maintenance costs
- 1.5% homeowners insurance, and $500 per month in condominium fees

From the rental side the assumptions are:

- 2% rent growth rate
- 5% investment return
- 2% inflation
- 1.5% renters insurance, and 1 month of security deposit

In this scenario, as long as the rent was under $2,350, renting is the better option.

Other Things to Consider

While the math on whether to buy or rent is important, it's not the end of this decision. There are other aspects you need to think about before you sign on the dotted line.

Income or Job

To buy a home, you would most likely need to take out a mortgage. A mortgage is a loan with monthly payments that have consequences when they go unpaid. For this reason, the stability of your job and income are very important considerations if you'd like to buy. You need the ability to keep making those payments, month in and month out.

If you're expecting that your pay will increase and you'll stay at that job or move to a similar job with ease, there's less reason to worry. If you're in an industry that changes quickly or working a job where the salary fluctuates every month (like sales), then you need to make sure you have enough saved up outside your normal pay periods so you won't miss a payment.

If you rent and you lose your job or your income drops, there are ways to move out to a cheaper place. With a purchased home, selling it and looking for a cheaper one would be a long process where you would still owe mortgage payments during the transition. Plus, rushing a real estate sale is never in the best interests of the seller.

Will You Stay?

Do you see yourself living in the same neighbourhood for longer than ten years? If so, buying becomes more attractive. Consider where your family lives, whether you like the weather, the area, the amenities as you age, etc. Certain neighbourhoods might be perfect for young 20 something's, but hell for those in their 40s with young children. If you're looking to buy, you would ideally want to live in a place that makes you happy at all ages.

If you plan on having children, there are even more things to consider like school quality in the area, distance to children's activities and community centres, etc.

Lastly, how set is your job's location? Would you be able to find a new job in your field in the area, or will you have to move if your company moves? What about a situation where you get an amazing offer across the country? Having a home would make that decision difficult.

The Mortgage

If you've gone through the above calculation and decided that buying a home is right for you, a mortgage probably is too. If you're one of the few people that can drop a few hundred thousand dollars in cash on something, you're probably not the type of person that needs this book. For everyone else, you'll need to borrow.

A mortgage is a large loan, generally paid over 30 years, at an interest rate that can be specified or chosen to be variable with whatever is happening in your local economy. The large time period creates a situation where on a $400,000 loan, you'll pay an additional $287,478 in interest over a 30 year period[9]. The name is derived from the French words meaning 'death pledge' apparently, so no surprises there. To avoid the huge interest amount, you could choose a shorter loan period, but you'll have to pay very large monthly payments. Most people deal with the interest.

Some vocabulary to start you off!

Principal: The amount of money you're borrowing. In our case, $400,000.

Interest: The rate at which you'll be borrowing this money. Rates are decided by the lender, generally a bank. The rate depends on the underlying interest rates in the economy as well as your individual credit score. Remember that thing? This is one of the few times it comes in handy.

Fixed Interest Rate: This is one of the simpler ones; the rate on your mortgage document will be the one you pay for the mortgage term. If it says 5%, that's what you'll pay every year. You should choose this option if you believe the interest rates will go up in the future.

Variable Interest Rate: If you think interest rates are bound to go down, you might want to go with this option. It allows the interest rate to fluctuate and adjust to whatever the economy's interest rates are doing. This is the riskier path, since the interest rates can fluctuate widely and you might find yourself in a situation where you can't pay a new (much higher) rate.

Down Payment: The initial amount of money you give the lender to show that you're good for the loan. It starts at 5%of the loan value, and goes up from there. It generally hovers around 20% though. We'll discuss why later.

Mortgage Term: The amount of time over which you agree to pay the agreed upon interest rate before you are re-assessed for a new one. This is generally a much shorter time than the full life of your mortgage loan because the bank wants to make bank on you and increase interest rates (that's their job!).

Amortization period: The amount of time in which the bank expects you to fully repay your loan. Generally around 30 years, but could be more or less depending on you and your bank.

Blended payments: This is the technical name for each monthly payment (or biweekly, whatever schedule you agree to). It's blended because the payment includes both interest payments and repayment of the principal amount.

Loan to Value Ratio (LTV): The ratio of the loan amount (how much you owe the bank) to the value of the asset you bought (your home's market value).

Mortgages are very complicated debt thingies, so much so that even people who have them don't fully understand what's going on or what they pay for every month. To deal with that, let's go through some examples to show how changing some variables will affect how much you pay.

Let's say you want to buy a house that costs $500,000 (a bargain in many of the more populated areas of our country). We'll deal with three different scenarios, changing only one variable.

Scenario One: Credit Score and Interest Rate
Your credit score will make a huge difference on how much you pay for a home. Let's say you either have an 'Excellent' or 'Fair' credit score, 770 or 640, respectively. You should also know that many banks won't lend to individuals with scores lower than Fair, or they'll charge outrageous interest rates if they do. You have to be very careful about your score if you want a mortgage. The

difference in rates between Excellent and Fair can be quite big, up to a percent and a half.

If an Excellent score will get you a rate of 4%, the amount of interest you'll pay on that $400,000 ($500,000 minus the 20% down payment) with a 5 year mortgage term on a 25 year amortization will be $305,581. Your monthly payment will be $2,104[10].

If a Fair score gets you a rate of 5.25%, the exact same mortgage will have you paying $413,344 in interest over the life of your loan, with a monthly payment of $2,384.

Pretty big difference as far as total interest goes, but not so much on a monthly basis. This is why some people don't even realize how much money they pay in interest over the life of their mortgages.

Scenario Two: Mortgage Amortization Period
How much time you take to pay down your loan will make a huge difference in your monthly payment. Let's see the difference between a common 25 year amortization period and a shorter 15 year period. Interest rate at 4% for both, 20% down, 5 year mortgage term, everything the same as before.

With a 25 year amortization period, the monthly payment will be $2,104 like we saw above.

At 15 years, the monthly payment goes up to $2,952! That's a huge difference to be paying every month, but doing this will save you$105,106 in interest, down to $200,475 from $305,581 over the life of your mortgage.

Scenario Three: Down payment
How much you decide to put down on a home makes a large difference to both the amount of interest you'll pay and the monthly payment, since the less you pay upfront the more money you'll be borrowing. On top of that, lower down payments trigger an additional insurance fee that must be paid. Let's say you'll put

either 20% or 5% as your down payment. That's either $100,000 or $25,000 that you need to come up with in cash.

In the 20% down payment situation, you'll have a $400,000 mortgage, with the same 4% interest, 25 year amortization, and 5 year term as before. This situation will cost you $2,104 monthly with $305,581 in total interest paid over the life of the loan.

At 5% down payment, the loan increases to $475,000, with the same terms as above. If we don't include the insurance fee, you'd be at a monthly payment of $2,499 and a total interest paid of $362,876. But in reality that insurance payment would add an additional $19,000 to your mortgage on top of the already increased mortgage amount[11], to a total monthly payment of $2,599. This increase could be worth it depending on your situation though.

Mortgage Default Insurance: Is it Worth it to Save Less for a Down Payment?

We just briefly discussed Mortgage Default Insurance (MDI) in the example above. This extra fee lets you lock down a loan without saving up as much cash as you would need for a traditional 20% down payment. The amount you pay for this privilege will vary from 2.80% to 4.00%[12] of your total mortgage amount depending on the size of the down payment. This amount can be bundled into your mortgage payment or paid up front.

Down payment (% of Home Price)	5%-9.99%	10%-14.99%	15%-19.99%	20% or Higher
Mortgage Default Insurance (% of Home Price)	4.00%	3.10%	2.80%	0.00%

If we keep using our $500,000 home example, putting only 5% down versus 20% down is a $75,000 difference in the amount of cash you need to save up before you can have a home. Sometimes it can be worth it, but it's a potentially precarious position.

Future Income

Are you not able to save the 20% down payment because you're in a depressed salary state right now? Then it might work out if you take your future income potential into account and make larger than necessary payments later on to reduce your mortgage to the point where the insurance goes away (typically a particular loan to value ratio set by the lender). However, when I say 'depressed salary state', I don't mean "I'm not making a lot of money right now but I just know I'll do better in a few years." What I mean is that you're in an MBA program, or are a medical student, or just starting out as a lawyer, careers that have exponential salary growth very quickly, more or less guaranteed. 5% annual raises are not enough for this type of argument, unless you think you'll save more in the future than you do now (unlikely, but if you take the next section to heart then maybe I can help you with that).

Appreciation in Value

Do you think home prices in the area going to skyrocket in a few years? Then it might be worth it to be pay the insurance off for a bit and then ask for an appraisal from your lender. This is where the loan to value ratio comes in again. The insurance payment may be cancelled or taken out of your mortgage at a certain loan to value ratio threshold, generally 78% LTV. If the home's value goes up a lot in a short period of time, that ratio will change on its own, regardless of how many payments you've made. This is a risky strategy though, since no one can predict housing markets.

Investment Property

Do you plan to flip this property or rent it out right after purchasing it? If so, it might be worthwhile to do some calculations. When you sell the property to someone else, the mortgage would get cancelled and paid back on that day (if your lender allows this), freeing you from the insurance payment as well. In this scenario the insurance payment is a short term expense and the return from the sale might be worth it. To figure out if that's the case, you'll have to do some math. The other option is renting out the place and being a landlord. We'll discuss this more in the investment section since this part is about the home you're actually going to be living in.

When Mortgage Default Insurance Might Not Be a Good Idea

Other than the whole 'paying extra because you're in a rush to buy something you can't afford' thing, in some scenarios mortgage insurance can be a pretty devastating addition to your mortgage payment.

Depreciation in Value

In the event of a housing decline in your area, the value of your home will tank. When that happens, your mortgage could potentially be larger than the value of the home. This creates the opposite of the appreciation situation above, where your LTV ratio will go the opposite way, creating a longer time period for you to pay down the insurance. This is what happened in 2008/2009 when the U.S. housing market crashed along with the stock market and people were paying their normal mortgage payments on houses that were worth much less. In these situations, even if they had sold their homes they would still owe the bank money.

Loss of Income

In the event that you lose your job or your pay drops, the higher payments that are part of this strategy will drag you down financially during your re-adjustment period looking for a new job. As we saw in the example before, the lower down payment and insurance added almost $500 every month to your expenses. Make sure that you'll be able to deal with that increased expense if something happens to your paycheque.

Debt
Why Do People Go Into Debt?
As of December 2016, Canadians have a debt level of $1.67 per $1 of disposable income[13]. That's huge! But why?

Generally, people go into debt because of four reasons:

Necessities
You need somewhere to live, a car to get you places, and potentially schooling to get a job. Debt relating to taking care of basic needs is generally the biggest portion of any household's debt because of how large mortgages are.

Lifestyle
Eating out and going on expensive vacations they can't afford are some of the ways that households can rack up debt due to their lifestyle. Some of these actions may be small but add up over time, like buying lunch every day. People also have a habit of using plastic for big ticket lifestyle items like plane tickets or designer clothing.

Life Situations
Getting married or having children has the potential to create higher than normal expenses for a year or so, which many households handle with debt. Temporary situations like unemployment where you may need to borrow money to support yourself are also covered in this debt category.

Legal Issues
Being bad at paying taxes or parking tickets can turn into a real issue if you don't pay attention or accidentally make a mistake. The CRA will charge you interest on any unpaid amounts plus penalties for trying to fool them, more on that in the taxes section ahead. If you ever need a lawyer for a will settlement or a divorce it can be very expensive and generally unforeseen, so you'll

probably have to come up with the money quickly. It's easy to go into debt when one of these situations arises.

Good Debt versus Bad Debt

According to popular opinion debt comes in two flavours, 'good debt' and 'bad debt'. 'Good debt' is debt incurred to buy something that will increase in value, or create an increase in value somewhere in your life. Education and home buying loans are generally included in this category.

Most of the time this makes sense. In theory, an education will make you more employable and increase potential earnings over your lifetime. Depending on the lender, student loans can have a low-ish interest rate, which tries not to hurt you too much financially. With home loans, it's a common belief that real estate always increases in value so the house you moved into 20 years ago would have gone up in price significantly since then, which makes it a great investment. This may or may not be true (see the investment section), but housing is generally a less risky asset because it has value as something you can use. The interest rates are the wildcard here, as they generally obey whatever economy you happen to be living in at the time of the loan.

Some people would also classify automobile loans as good debt. I would disagree unless the car is absolutely essential to your work (a contractor needs a truck, for example). A commuting vehicle alone would not qualify, since cars are a depreciating asset and therefore don't fit the rule that good debt must create an appreciation in value. 'A car loses 30% of its value the minute you drive it off the lot' is a common saying for a reason.

Bad debt is everything else. Credit cards, auto loans, etc. The worst of the worst are cash advance and payday loans. These loans are often called predatory, as their main client base is less wealthy and generally lives paycheque to paycheque, requiring loans for any emergencies. Payday loans will give you small amounts of money, a few hundred dollars to a thousand, for a few days or a week. You'll get charged the equivalent of 300% annual interest for these loans with additional fees. Stay as far away from these as you can!

Debt could also be called financing. When you go to buy a big ticket item like a car or furniture, sometimes the dealership or store will offer to give you a loan. Should you take it?

Is Financing a Bad Idea?

0% interest for 6 months! You've seen these signs at car dealerships all over the place I'm sure. But is getting something using seller offered financing a good idea?

Generally, no. Very few people will be disciplined enough (or have the cash) to actually pay the whole thing off when that promotional rate or free period ends. And when it ends, boy are you in trouble. If the loan isn't paid off, the creditor will usually back charge all the interest from the beginning of the deal, making it extremely lucrative for the seller. These deals hinge on the fine print, and not reading it closely can cost you large amounts of money. These companies are businesses first, and businesses need to make money.

Debt Reduction Techniques

If you're serious about wiping out any debt that you currently carry, there are two main schools of thought on how to do it. One skews more emotional and one is more math based. As long as you're motivated to reduce your debt or eliminate it completely, which method you use is really up to you.

Snowball Technique

This method of reducing debt works by exploiting human nature's love of short term gratification. With this method, you pay all your minimum payments first, and then focus any extra money on eliminating the smallest debt. Once the first debt is paid off, you apply all extra money to the next smallest debt and work your way up as you zero out smaller debts. This method boosts motivation from the small wins and allows you to keep going as you reduce the number of debts you have. This method is very effective, but it generally incurs more interest which could be detrimental with large balances or high interest rates.

Highest Interest Rate First (Avalanche Technique)

After minimum payments, this approach focuses all extra money on the debt with the highest interest rate first. Doing it this way will reduce the amount of interest you pay overall which will allow you to pay down your debts faster on the whole. However, it could be that it will take you longer to repay that first debt, giving you less of a motivation boost to pay off the rest. This could lead to less of a drive to pay down your debts.

Before deciding on a debt repayment strategy, you should weigh your personality type and decide if you need the extra motivation that comes from the Snowball Technique or are disciplined enough to use the Avalanche Method.

Let's go through an example to show the impact of using either route. We have $10,000 in debt, split among 5 debts.
- Debt A: $500 at 2% interest, $20 minimum payment
- Debt B: $1,000 at 4%, $30 minimum payment
- Debt C: $2,000 at 5%, $50 minimum payment

- Debt D: $2,500 at 10%, $75 minimum payment
- Debt E: $4,000 at 20%, $110 minimum payment

You have $1,000 every month left over in your budget to go after your debts.

Using the Avalanche Method, you will be debt free in 11 months, having paid $431 in interest. Using the Snowball Method, you'll be done in 12 months, having paid $787 in interest. That's a $356 difference[14], but if it's the difference between getting discouraged or not, it's worth it! The differences between the two methods can vary and are most pronounced in situations where the debts are large or the interest rates are high.

Debt Reduction Plan

After you've chosen a debt reduction technique that works with your personality, what are the next steps to get rid of debt?

The first thing to do is to make a list prioritizing all outstanding debt using the method you chose above. After that you must decide if you're responsible enough to keep your credit cards around. If your debt is student or mortgage-y in nature, this may not be an issue. But, if you've accumulated credit card debt, it might be a different story. Institute a strict dollar value or type of expense restriction for using credit, if you feel that you are responsible enough. An example would be spending only $200 per month on credit or only on legitimate emergencies, like unexpected car repairs. If you feel you cannot be trusted with the cards or you've failed to follow your own rules, cut up the cards (you can always get news one when you're ready). Freezing them in a block of opaque ice works too. The point is not to get into any more debt than you have to while repaying your old ones.

The next step is dumping any savings you have onto the debt, making sure to leave a small emergency fund. This is not possible for everyone; some people are using this book to build savings in the first place! Regardless of savings, the next step is creating a timeline for becoming debt free using current budgeted savings per month. Lay out a biweekly or monthly timeline, and plot when you'll be able to rid yourself of each one of your debts if you kept going at your current pace. If you want to alter your budget in order to save more money and pay down the debt faster, plot another timeline on top of the existing one with the new savings amounts. Having the two together is a great way to motivate yourself to save more money since it's a visual reminder of the difference every saved dollar makes.

If the timeline to debt freedom is still too slow for your liking and you're saving as much as you possibly can, it may be time to look for a part-time job or do some overtime at work. Do you have any transferable skills for temporary work in a small business or retail? If not, a pizza delivery or Uber driving career could be just what you need to get your debt under control.

When additional work is not possible, either due to time commitments or an already 14 hour work day (been there, done that), you can turn to selling items that you no longer need. The money this selling will bring in won't be as good as getting another job, but when your main goal in life is to get out of debt every little bit counts.

Emotions and Debt

People deal with debt differently. Some people are anxious about paying it off and not owing anybody anything, even if the debt is the 'good' kind. For these people, paying off whatever debt they have can be much more fulfilling than saving and investing, even if the math shows that investing is the better choice. That's fine. Personal finance is just that, personal.

On the other hand, there are people that are not bothered by debt at all, treating it as just a part of life. While this approach creates less stress for the individual, it normalizes debt and could lead to taking on more of it.

The most important thing about debt is realizing that for a majority of debt holders, debt is a choice. You don't have to buy a house, a car, and a vacation to Hawaii if you don't have the income to support it. Renting, using the bus, and camping are perfectly valid alternatives. By owning your choices and realizing that credit is not to be taken lightly, you'll become a more thoughtful human being with less financial problems.

Student Debt

Student debt is starting to become one of the few types of debt that is more or less unavoidable these days as university and college tuition costs rise. Education debt is often considered to be one of the 'good' debts we discussed above since it can be an investment. But it's only an investment if you treat it like one.

Research, forward thinking, and analysis are essential to deciding whether an investment is a good idea for you. You should do the same thing if you're considering taking on debt for school.

Should You Go into Debt for School?

Don't go into debt for schooling if your reasons for choosing a school or a major are any of the following:

'My parents told me to go here/take this major.'
'I just randomly picked this school/major.'
'The buildings are really pretty and it's a chill atmosphere.'
'I need to go to university/college, what else would I do?'

These are all bad reasons to make a decision that has the potential to follow you for the rest of your life and screw up your credit until you pay it off. That could take two years, or it could take twenty. It's one of the few debts that even bankruptcy won't save you from, so be very sure about this decision. Before you make this decision, think about how long you want to be responsible for this debt, since there may be others in your future as well, like a mortgage and/or a car payment.

To make the debt worth it, you'll need to assess what your job prospects will be once you graduate. This will show you how fast you'll be able to pay off the debt. Research entry level pay in your field for both the best and worst case scenarios, job hunting wise. Do the math. Figure out how long it would take to pay down the debt and what kind of work you'd be doing in both scenarios. You can also consider if you'd be better off delaying your attendance or not going to school at all given the costs. Some jobs that don't require a degree pay pretty well, I hear.

Example time! Let's assume that you go to a business school which costs $6,500 the first year and $14,000 for the next three years. This can be low or high, depending on what part of the country you go to school in, but it's what I paid. You can major in accounting, finance, or general business. The first two have specialized jobs available to graduates. In a graduating class of 500, 300 are general business graduates and 100 each are part of the accounting and finance majors.

If you were to borrow your entire tuition, you would graduate with a debt of $48,000. With an assumed interest rate of 4%, how long would it take you to pay off this debt?

Let's talk assumptions first, since there are a lot of them in this example. We're assuming you live in a place where you can get by on $20,000 per year. There are no house or car purchases, taxes, or emergencies in this fake universe.

Accounting Majors
The specialized job in this case is auditing, where demand is high and spaces relatively low. The starting salary is $45,000. It goes up to $52,000 and $60,000 in the second and third years as you progress in the career. If you don't get the accounting job, you can look for other related jobs or compete with the general business major population for non-accounting business jobs which pay $35,000.

Probability of you landing this auditor job: 30 people out of the graduating class will get the coveted auditor position, so your chance within your graduating class is 30/100, or 30%, of making the cut. After living expenses you're left with $25,000 to put towards your debt and associated interest. You'll be able to pay the debt off in one year and ten months[15] with this career path.

Finance Majors
With finance the number of people who get the ideal jobs, equity research and investment banking, is even lower. It's somewhere around 10/100 or 10% of a graduating class. Let's say these jobs

pay $80,000 for the first year with $20,000 increases each year. If you're one of the lucky few who succeed you can pay off your debt in ten months. Otherwise you are again competing with the general business graduates for those $35,000 a year jobs.

General Business Majors
What about the general business graduates? They have a higher chance of getting employed due to the larger job market for their skills, but the salaries are lower than the specialized majors. Let's say they get paid $35,000 with 5% increases every year. If they spend the same $20,000 a year as the other people in these examples, they only have $15,000 per year to put towards their loans. It'll take them three years and three months to pay down their loans!

I guess what I'm trying to say with this example is that it'll be substantially harder to pay down debt if your education is not specialized with a potential for higher income. However, those roles are also less common and the competition for them is fierce. Before you decide to take on debt to go to school, you should consider whether you can cut it in a more competitive and more lucrative career, no matter what you decide to study. It can also be beneficial to go to school a year later if it means you took the time to work and save up the money instead of borrowing.

That was pretty involved wasn't it? This is the kind of analysis that shows you're taking schooling and its financial implications seriously. To research, you should look at websites like Glassdoor and LinkedIn to see what kinds of jobs your major can get you. Some schools publish information about the average salary upon graduation of their students. Try to speak to alumni outside of alumni events (those events are highly biased), and with people in the industry you're interested in, preferably before you even start school. Schooling is a big decision that affects the rest of your life and shouldn't be taken lightly.

Is a Pricey University Worth it?

This depends entirely on the results of your research. What does your industry of choice need from you in order to give you a job? There are some industries where a brand name school is the only way to get in. If that's your case, and the math works out for repaying the higher debt, cautiously go for it. If your career choice will accept a type of degree regardless of it came from, the cheaper the school the better. Education is quickly becoming a luxury purchase these days. Don't buy it if you don't need it.

Net Worth

Net Worth is a number that's supposed to convey your financial worth and well-being. It's fairly easy to calculate. In general, net worth is your assets less your liabilities or debt. If you have lots of debt and little assets your net worth could be negative.

Assets are the financial and non-financial things you own: a home, retirement accounts, bank accounts, savings accounts, a car, even a boat if you have one. Anything you can sell or trade for money.

Liabilities or debts are just that, your mortgage and any debts you might have. These debts include credit cards, student loans, lines of credit, and any other money you owe to anybody in your personal life.

Let's look at two different people. Maya and Michelle are sisters. Maya has the following assets:
- $5,000 in her savings account
- $400,000 house
- $10,000 car

Her debts are:
- $7,000 in credit card balances
- $390,000 mortgage
- An auto loan of $9,000

Her net worth is $9,000.

Michelle has:
- $10,000 in her savings accounts
- $1,000 emergency fund
- A $1,000 balance on her credit card

She doesn't own her house or a car. Michelle's net worth is $10,000.

Remember that the people who seem to have it all don't always. Many of those things they show off are acquired with debt, which people on the outside can't see.

2 Budgets and Saving

What is Budgeting and Saving?

Saving is the act of avoiding spending money today in order to spend it later. The definition makes it sound so easy, but it's putting it in motion and sticking to a plan that's hard for most people.

If I make $2,000 a month, but only really need $1,500 (for rent and food), I can use the $500 to either buy something in the future (a car, a house, life in retirement), or I can use it now on things that would be nice to have (a new shirt, a bottle of wine, a concert). This is the main decision you'll have to make when trying to save money: what is more important to you? Maybe that concert is a once in a lifetime chance to see a favourite artist, but is it worth one week of retirement spending? The savings versus spending decision is all about what is 'worth it' to you. Some people want to have a super nice car, other people want to retire at 35 (stay tuned for more on that possibility later), and some place a lot of importance on going to restaurants as often as possible because that's what they love to do. None of these decisions are inherently better than the others. Just remember there are trade offs for everything in life and they apply here too.

For example, it's very unlikely that you'll be able to do all three of those things. unless you make several hundred thousand dollars a year, in which case I'm very jealous.

Budgeting is what allows you to be able to highlight the things that are important to you, and de-emphasize the things that aren't. This process lets spending to be allocated to important things and downplays not so important things.

A budget is a system that keeps track of your income and spending, usually in particular categories which we'll talk about later. The budget itself can be anything from super complex Excel spreadsheets that you create yourself, or a free online service that

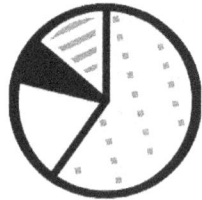

catalogues everything for you. I'll provide you with a simplified version of what I use later on as well as some easier options.

How Much to Save

The age-old question, what is the minimum amount of money I have to save to be okay in the future and still enjoy the best life I can now?

Like I said before, this entirely depends on what you want out of life. If you're comfortable working until 65 or over and never owning a nice house or car, you should be able to get by with saving very little. But very few people want that type of life, so you're going to need to put away at least a little bit every month.

I focus on retirement, housing, and a vehicle because those are large and expensive items that most people are interested in having in their lives. This section is not about saving up for an annual trip or a designer piece of clothing, but you could apply the same methods to those smaller saving goals too.

Before you decide what your goals are, consider the assumptions you're making about the future. The majority of people expect the current retirement system to stay in place with the same benefits, with the Canada Pension Plan (CPP) and Old Age Security providing you a small safety net when you retire. This may or may not be true in 50 years, who knows what the future looks like. If you're working right now, your employer is taking mandatory CPP deductions from your pay in order to provide older Canadians with retirement income if they can't provide it for themselves. The future is unpredictable, but with demographic shifts towards more middle-aged and older people than young ones to replace them, it's possible that the system will work less efficiently or stop altogether by the time you're ready to retire. Might want to save a bit more for retirement, just in case.

Potentially depressing future aside, let's work on some examples that will depress you even further. Let's say I want all three of those things. A nice house in a nice suburb of a big city, a nice new car, and retirement at 60 instead of 65. It's math time!

If I'm 25 now and I want to have the nice house and car by age 30, how much money do I need to save every month to achieve my three dreams?

A nice home in York Region (the suburbs around Toronto) averages around $758,000 as of March 2015[16]. This is the average of all housing types, but you're probably going to want a detached home or townhouse, which will set you back even more. In most home-buying situations, you'll be putting 20% down and paying the rest as a mortgage. We'll only account for the 20% here, since that's immediate cash coming out at age 30.

20% of $758,000 is $151,600. If I'm saving up every month for these 5 years, I'll need to save $1,329 every month and find a bank that would pay me 2% interest[17]. After that, I'll still have to pay $3,190 every month for the mortgage on a 25 year 5 year term 4% mortgage. Holy moly.

Now the car. I'm a fan of the Tesla Model S, which after incentives costs $76,400 cash, or $9,170 for a down payment on a loan of $808 per month for 8 years. If I buy it outright at age 30, I'll need to save $670 every month at that same 2% rate, assuming the Tesla will cost the same in 5 years. If I want to go for the loan, I'll only need to save $80 every month in order to get to that down payment, but then my monthly payments will increase by $808 for 8 years.

Retirement time. This is the most loosey goosey portion of anybody's planning because no one has any idea what life will be like in 35 years. But let's say that I think I can live on $30,000 a year in retirement (this is an arbitrary figure and is entirely up to what kind of retirement you want. If you think you're going to be a globetrotting grandma or grandpa, you're going to need some more moolah). Let's say I want to retire at 60 and I think I'll live until 92. According to the website I'm using, I'll need to save $351 a month assuming I can get a return of 6% after inflation, both during the 35 years of saving and the 32 years of retirement[18]. How you get to 6% will be discussed in the investment section later.

To sum up, if you want all these things, you'll have to save either $2,351 per month in the option where you buy the car outright, or $1,762 if you pay for it with a loan later. The difference now will come out of future payments, so the choice is up to you. You should also be mindful of the future monthly expenses that come with the mortgage and car loan that would reduce any savings potential in the future, $3,190 or $3,998 are huge monthly bills!

Pretty big numbers huh. Either of those monthly savings figures is probably about half your monthly income, if not more. How does that feel? Probably terrifying. The good news is that if you're reading this book, you're already interested in getting started. The most important thing about achieving these goals is time.

If you take 10 years to get to the house and car instead of 5, you'll only have to save $819 per month ($352 retirement, $310 for the down payment, and $156 for the car outright), or $681 per month if you take a car loan. This is using the same 2% interest rate, so why is there such a big difference in the amounts?

Compound Interest

Whoever said cash is king didn't know about compound interest. Compound interest is the concept that the interest or return you earn on an investment each year is added to your initial investment, and in the second year that return or interest is calculated on the new larger amount, increasing the money you make on the investment faster every year. It's a bit confusing without seeing it, so here's an example:

Year 1: I have 1,000, I put it in the bank at 2%.
By the end of this year I'll have $1,000 + $20 in interest to a balance of $1,020 at the end of the year.
Year 2: $1,020 *2%=$20.4, which gets added for a yearend balance of $1,040.40
Year 3: $1,040.4*2%=$20.81, which gets added for a yearend balance of $1,061.21
Year 4: $1,061.21*2%=$21.22, which gets added for a yearend balance of $1,082.43
Year 5: $1,082.43*2%=$21.65, which gets added for a yearend balance of $1,104.08

Without compound interest, the original $1,000 would only increase by $20 per year for 5 years to end up with $1,100. $4 is not a big difference, but $1,000 is not a lot of money either. Let's look at it from a more realistic approach. Say you've used all the savings knowledge you'll learn in the next section and have $20,000 to invest every year for 5 years. If you put it in an investment that earns 6% instead of in a bank account, after 5 years you'll have $119,506 instead of $100,000[19]. Not too shabby.

The key to taking advantage of compound interest is *time*. 5 years is nothing. If you're reading this you're probably a young person. Let's assume you're 25 and plan to retire like most people at 65. That's 40 years of time for compound interest to do its magic. Saving $10,000 per year and investing it at 6% for 40 years is going to get you$1,650,477[20]. Why wouldn't you start saving with numbers like that?

How Much to Save: Part 2

The 10% Rule, What is it and Should I Really Save That Much?

'Save 10% of your income every year and you'll be fine for retirement' is what you always hear from parents or financial advisors. But does the math check out? Do you really need to save that much? Or even scarier, do you need to save more?

This question requires a bit of math, and I know how much you like that, but it's necessary to really understand what's going on. Example time!

Shannon is a 25 year old marketing specialist making $45,000 a year (we're going to ignore taxes because they make math annoying). When she retires at 65, she wants to have $45,000 to spend each year. In order to spend $45,000 for 27 years (let's assume a 92 year life span), she needs $1,498,782 when she turns 65 in order to have that lifestyle, assuming a return of 6% (after inflation) in both retirement and savings periods. If Shannon saves 10% of her income per year, $4,500 for 40 years, she ends up with $1,004,544[21]. That's not quite what she was looking for. To get to her goal, Shannon needs to save $6,720 a year, or 14.9% of her income.

John is a 25 year old software engineer who makes $80,000 a year. He also hopes to spend $45,000 in retirement. Using the same assumptions, he also needs $1,498,782 at 65 to retire. But if he saves 10% of his income at $8,000 a year, he ends up with $1,801,711 at age 65. He needs less than 10%, 8.4% to be precise.

What have we learned from these examples so far? If you're planning to retire on an income similar to the one you have right now, you'll likely need to save more than 10%. If you're happy to retire on less than your current income, you'll need to save less than 10%. But what about when you start saving?

Michelle is a 30 year old lawyer who makes $80,000 a year. She would like to spend $45,000 in retirement like John and Shannon. If she saves 10%, she can get to $1,288,942 by age 65.

Five years sure makes a big difference, the difference between saving only 8.4% of your income and having to save 11.63%.

The earlier you get on the road to saving for your goals, the less you'll have to save due to the magic of compound interest.

Do note that all the calculations above assumed that you'll be saving and investing in an RRSP account and include income from the Canada Pension Plan and Old Age Security. Whether you would like to account for those payments or not is up to you.

Free Money

A majority of employers will offer to 'match' your contribution to retirement savings if you invest with the company's chosen provider, up to a point. As you've already learned, this only applies to Defined Contribution Pension Plans.

Generally, you'll have to agree to put 5% of your income away into this savings plan and the company will match some of the contribution. Regardless of how much the company matches, it's likely that you should contribute either the maximum allowed amount or the most you can personally save, whichever is lower.

The nice thing about a company match is that it's automatic, meaning you don't have to do anything extra to save more money except sign a form when you want to start contributing! The money will come out of your paycheque and you'll never know it was there. This type of automation is the holy grail of saving without pain, since you never even see the money. Out of sight, out of (spendy) mind.

While this sounds very rosy, there are some instances where you may want to be hesitant to contribute the full amount, and may want to run some numbers to make sure it's still a good deal. These situations deal with the investments available in the company plan and a low employer match percentage. If the choice of investments within the plan is limited, or none of the investments make sense with your investment preferences (more on these in the investing section, up next!), it could be that you're better off doing your own thing. It could also be that the employer match is quite low, maybe at 1% to every 5% you put in. In that situation, it could also be worth doing some math to decide whether investing without your company match makes sense or not, since bad investment options and a low company match might eliminate any benefit from the match

Emergency Fund

Before you start having big dreams of houses, fancy cars, and a retirement of traveling the world, you might need an emergency fund.

An Emergency Fund is an amount of money you keep easily accessible that could carry you through a typical unemployment period in your field or an unexpected emergency. Some people will need more than others. A common rule of thumb is three to six months of bare minimum living expenses, but you should adjust according to how quickly it would take you to find another job if you quit or are fired.

If you invest your emergency fund, make sure to invest in something with a very low risk profile (more on that later), since an emergency will require the funds regardless of how you feel about any investment gains or losses. Most advice will tell you to keep it in a high interest savings account.

If you feel that your job is very steady or you could get a new job within two weeks, it's possible that an emergency fund may not be for you. This is also the case if your living expenses are minimal (if you live with the parents for example). How much to keep in this kind of fund is a very personal decision that's heavily dependent on the unique factors of your situation.

You should also consider non-job related emergencies when deciding how much to keep in an emergency fund. How likely is it that you'll need expensive elective medical procedures that your insurance might not cover? Braces, Root Canals, and prescription drugs can be quite expensive. Emergency home repairs like burst pipes or a bad car crash are good examples too.

Some people might have an issue with keeping thousands of dollars in a bank account barely earning interest. That's understandable, since the same amount of money can be invested and reap rewards. However, it's important to understand the emergency fund's purpose is to rescue you in a crisis. The emergency fund is insurance, and when has insurance ever paid you interest or dividends?

Where to Save

Now that you know how much to save for your goals, where do you put the money?

We just talked about an emergency fund, but you should do something else with your money before you even go there. Pay off high interest debt! The waterfall chart below shows you where money should go at the beginning of your saving journey (at the top) and how to proceed over time to the more advanced levels of saving once you've mastered or maxed out the one above it.

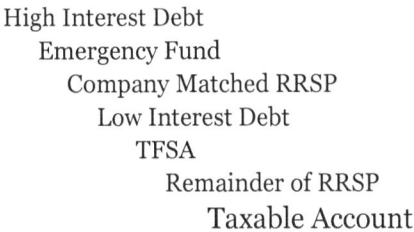

> High Interest Debt
> Emergency Fund
> Company Matched RRSP
> Low Interest Debt
> TFSA
> Remainder of RRSP
> Taxable Account

High Interest Debt

Credit card debt, and sometimes car loans, fall into this category. Anything above 10% interest is high interest debt in my mind. You have no business investing anywhere if you're carrying this kind of debt and not paying it down as soon as possible. Priority number one is getting this bucket to $0.

Emergency Fund

This money should be kept in a high interest savings account so that if an emergency happens you'll be able to deal with it immediately. Keep this as big or small as your situation requires and preferably separate from your other money so that there are no temptations to use it in non-emergencies.

Company Matched RRSP

The free money we talked about earlier. If your employer offers a match larger than half of your contribution, and the selections available to you are acceptable, put in the maximum required contribution into the employer's Pension Plan. You may want to put any remaining savings into the buckets below or keep all your savings up to the maximum RRSP limit (see below) in the employer's plan if you're extremely happy with the investment selection.

Low Interest Debt

Whether you choose to pay off debt or invest is a touchy and personal subject, depending on how you feel about having debt and what the interest rate is. Anywhere from 0-5% interest rate is a toss-up between investing and paying it down due to the market on average returning 7% over the long term. This return is not guaranteed in any given year, with some years having huge market losses, so it really depends on your comfort level. The idea is that you could potentially earn more by investing than you would by paying down the loan. If the market returns 7% in the long term and you're choosing to pay down a 3% interest loan you'd only be earning 3%. But for a person who hates being in debt, debt free certainty will trump that mathematical maybe any day.

Tax Free Savings Account (TFSA)

This is a relatively new investment account the government created in 2009. The idea is that you put after tax money in the account (there is no tax credit for contributing), and any money you take out of the account will be tax free. If you were 18 or older in 2009 you'd have been able to contribute $52,000 by December 31, 2017. The annual contribution limit changes with who's in power in the government but for most of the account's life the limit was $5,500 per year, including 2017. The contribution room carries over every year, meaning if you've never contributed but have room available, you can put the entire amount into the account in that year, regardless of the annual maximum.

The name 'Savings Account' is very misleading, since you should really be using this account to invest in order to make the most out of the tax free withdrawals.

For young people, this account is generally a better place to put money as opposed to an RRSP because of the assumption that your salary will grow as you get older. In that case, saving RRSP contributions until later will give you a bigger tax break. That being said, if you run out of room in the TFSA and it's between not putting money in at all or the RRSP, go for the RRSP.

Registered Retirement Savings Plan (RRSP)

The most common retirement investing account in Canada. The idea here is that you put in pre-tax money (you get a tax deduction, more on that in the taxes section). Any money you withdraw will be taxed as regular income when you take it out. The annual contribution limit is 18% of your income or $26,010 (2017 amount), whichever is lower. The limit here is also cumulative like the TFSA; anything you don't use today can be carried forward to be used later. Hence why it can be better to use this account later on in life, when you're facing a larger tax bill because you're making a ton of money. You may take money out whenever you wish until age 71, when the RRSP must be converted into something called a Registered Retirement Income Fund (RRIF). This approach is not recommended because they have very strict withdrawal requirements.

The name 'Savings Account' is misleading here too, since you should be investing this money as well. There are some investments that do better in a RRSP versus TFSA and vice versa which we'll discuss later in the investment section.

Taxable Account

At this point you're a pro, maxing out all your tax-advantaged accounts. Where to next? The taxable investment account.

There are no perks of using this account. Anything you make here gets taxed in the year it happens. This is a very advanced account for people who are serious about saving and want to invest their savings even without tax breaks. Some investments do better here than in a TFSA or RRSP if you're maxed out and we'll talk about that later too.

Budgeting

You know how much to save and where to save it, but how do you actually go about saving? This is where budgeting comes in. A budget relies on the idea that every dollar you earn has a job to do, whether that's to feed you, house you, or be used in your retirement. But before we talk about how to budget, let's discuss why most people fail at budgeting and how to avoid these pitfalls.

No Accurate Record Keeping

If you don't know how much you're spending, how do you plan on changing it?

Many people start a budget without having any previous records of spending, meaning they're walking in blind without any knowledge of how much they should really be spending. A budget without previous spending data is just wishful thinking. There are many expenses that you don't really think about when you're setting goals, but spend on nonetheless. Small things like coffee or an automatic subscription are commonly forgotten items.

Creating a budget with no past information could also make the budget too restrictive and too idealistic. You could be super excited to save money at the beginning of the month, but then find yourself going over the budget you've projected and rage quitting because you set the bar too high. Budgets are much easier created than followed, so it's best to build them on a solid base.

It could also be that people are afraid of what they'll find when they look at their spending habits. They know they've been bad with their money, but don't want it spelled out for them. Well, acknowledgment is the first step to getting your things in order, so let's do it together.

To overcome this issue, I want you to track your spending for a while before you start budgeting.

Unattainable or Undefined Goals

The other main issue is that you want to save, but you don't know what you're saving for. This creates an aimless situation where saving ends up not being important, since there's no real reason you're doing it. Even seemingly specific goals like 'pay off all my debt' or 'save for a down payment' can be too broad for some people.

Timing is also key. You could have a very good specific goal, but without putting a timeline on it you might be giving yourself too much leeway in achieving that goal. Without a timeframe, something that would take six months to achieve could take a year or longer, leading to disappointment with the budget (which again could lead to quitting).

To overcome this issue, you should use specific dollar figures as often as possible in your goal setting and put a time constraint on those goals to really motivate you to achieve them.

No Adjustments

Budgets should be active documents; one month is rarely going to be the same as the one before it. Some events (like birthdays and major holidays) require more financial planning, and it's common for preferences and spending habits to change over time. A budget that doesn't account for these changes and fluctuations won't be useful, since you'd be judging yourself against artificial targets that are no longer relevant.

People assume budgets should be restrictive and forbid you from doing the things you want in order to save money. It doesn't have to be this way. If you love Chinese food, you put that Kung Pao Chicken in the budget. Purposeful and aware spending is the initial goal of a budget. If you want to save money on top of that, fantastic.

Every once in a while, you should take a look at your budget and see which categories you're always going over or under in and adjust them accordingly. When changes like a new job or new goals happen in your life, your budget should be adjusted too

Friends or Significant Other Are Not on Board

Even if you're really into the whole savings thing, if the person you love isn't or your friends aren't, you're going to have a hard time keeping it up. Peer pressure is a difficult thing to overcome. You'll have to either discuss budgeting and finances with these people and hope they can support you, or try to keep your resolve while hanging out with them. It's relatively easy to avoid buying five drinks at the club if you only go once a month, but much more difficult if that's where you hang out every weekend.

To try to deal with this issue, have the money talk with your people and see how they feel about these new priorities. They might even surprise you and start saving too.

Impatience

Budgets are not a magic Band-Aid. You won't go from broke to millionaire in one month of budgeting. You'll need to get into the groove of judging yourself every month and seeing where the money actually goes versus where you thought it was going. It takes time to adjust the budget to the real life situations that you couldn't have predicted when you initially put it together. It also takes time for the saved money to accumulate and be worth the effort. Budgeting is like working out, it's a new behaviour that must be learned and maintained. It usually takes at least a month of working hard to make the change. Give yourself a few months and allow for adjustments.

There's not much you can do to deal with this issue other than be patient and not give up when you inevitably get frustrated in the first few months of budgeting.

Overcomplication and Overachievement

If you come up with a massive, complicated spreadsheet to track your expenses and financial goals, it would be an exhausting exercise just to record spending so you might be less likely to use it. Keep the budget simple and it'll be easier to keep it updated. The less extra work it makes you do, the more likely you are to stick with it.

Overachievers also have trouble with budgeting. Some might want to take everything unnecessary out of your life and live like monks in order to pay off student loans as quickly as possible. For most people, that's not sustainable. You might burn out and go back to your old ways even harder than before, which is extremely counterproductive. You see this type of behaviour with people who have lost a lot of weight and then go right back up to, or even over, their old weight as if nothing happened.

Budgets don't suck. But people sometimes suck at making them or sticking to them. Budgets are a new habit and therefore must be introduced slowly and consistently until they stick. Huge changes are unlikely to happen overnight; don't get overwhelmed and just take it one day at a time.

Before You Start

Good budgets take some prep time before they reach maximum usefulness. You need to have categories that are relevant to the way you as an individual spend your money, and knowledge of your spending in each category.

Tracking

Like we just discussed, the primary reason budgets fail are because of bad planning, not knowing what you actually spend money on. To combat that, before you start a budget you should track all your spending for some time in order to have a solid base for a budget.

To start, get your credit card and bank statements for the last three months. Take a look at all the transactions and try to categorize them based on common budget line items. Things like shelter, food, entertainment, etc. Once you've done that, analyze whether you're comfortable with the total spending in each category. Make some decisions regarding where to reduce spending in order to meet the savings goals you made earlier.

By checking all your accounts, you might also notice some recurring charges that you forgot about or no longer need. This would be a good time to cancel these. It's also a good time to try to renegotiate any subscriptions or monthly payments that you might be able to reduce. This includes your phone, cable, internet, and any other services that you pay for.

If you only spend cash and don't keep receipts, this will be more difficult since there's no record of your spending. You may want to skip to the next step and do it for a longer period of time to get the best history you can.

Keep in mind any annual or infrequent expenses that you might have forgotten about. Car maintenance, home repairs, membership fees, and holiday gifts are all examples of large expenses that might only occur once or twice a year. If you're not

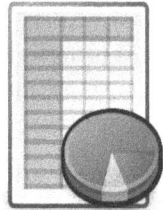

tracking your spending in the months they occur, they might be forgotten.

Once you have a decent idea of where past spending was going, it's time to do the heavy research. For a month or more, track every dollar you spend. It doesn't matter if you spent it through cash, credit, or debit. It doesn't matter if you think an item was a one-time event. Track and record every dollar. You might be surprised to see some spending that you weren't expecting, or some that you don't even notice on a day to day basis. You might also be surprised at how many items you thought were a one-time thing, but weren't (chocolate bars at the grocery store checkout are my guilty pleasure).

With all this information, sit down and start creating a budget based on what you've seen yourself spend and how you're interested in changing it. The funny thing is, you'll probably spend less in that month of tracking transactions just because you were in the mindset of thinking about your spending.

When you're making the initial budget, give yourself a bit of extra cushion for over ambition. You'll need it. It might also be useful to phase out the expenses you want to lower, working on a new area each month so you're not overwhelmed with a complete change in behaviour overnight. Some people find it more useful to create habits by going cold turkey, and some people prefer a more gradual change. Do what feels right for you. It's important that you feel comfortable with your budget and can carry it out. It needs to be challenging, but not impossible.

Ready, Set, Go
Budgeting Categories

After you've done the research, you're ready to create your budget. Most budgets follow a particular structure: they have the items that relate to a certain category of expenses and columns indicating how much you've spent and whether you've met your goals.

The categories most people use in their budgets are pretty standardized and broad, but feel free to get creative if your life inspires it. Remember that there's nothing inherently wrong with spending money on things that make you happy, regardless of what those things are. If wearing the latest clothes or playing the latest video games makes you happy, it goes in the budget.

Housing

Housing expenses usually take the form of rent or mortgage payments (interest and principal). Some people would include their home or renter's insurance costs and property tax in here as well. Utility costs may also be included here if they're relatively small and you're not particularly interested in changing them.

Transportation

How do you get where you need to go? If you own or lease a car, any car payments, car insurance, and gas will also go in this category. Everything that relates to getting you from point A to point B can be included here, to give you a full idea of how much your car costs you. Maintenance, carwashes, small car related items, everything. If you take public transportation, the cost of monthly passes or fares should be included. If you regularly take cabs, you should also account for it here. For example, if you know you plan to go out once a week and will require a cab home, your budget should reflect that.

Food (Groceries and Eating Out)

For most people, these need to be two distinct categories with their own allocated dollars. It'll be easier to notice your eating habits if the two types of food consumption are separate. Groceries should include all the consumable items bought for cooking at home, which doesn't include kitchen appliances or gadgets, only stuff that gets used up in the cooking process. This includes oils, foils and parchments, spices, and of course the actual food items like vegetables and meats.

In the eating out category, think about how many times a month you'd like to go out for food. This includes your morning coffee and breakfast, any lunches you don't pack, and dinners out. Then assign an average price per portion to each type of meal and calculate the amount you want to spend each month. This will be a guessing game for the first few months.

TV, Phone, and Internet

I can't live without my phone and internet connections, you probably feel the same. Monthly payments to the phone and internet companies belong in this category. Modem and connection fees should be included as well. If you paid extra to get a specific phone model, ditto. Same goes for cable TV or special channel premiums. You can make a judgment call on whether you want to put Netflix, HBO GO, Amazon Prime, etc. here or in the entertainment section of your budget.

Entertainment

I would personally put the above-mentioned content services here. They're more of a discretionary item than a monthly requirement and can usually be canceled at any time. Other than getting your TV fix, this category will include concert tickets, video games, books, movie tickets, anything you do to entertain yourself that costs money.

Household Expenses

Everybody needs toilet paper and toothpaste (or at least I hope so). These everyday items belong here. This category will include things like new towels for your bathroom, toothbrushes, cooking utensils, cleaning supplies, etc. Many people underestimate this category because they don't realize how often they buy paper towels or how expensive a vacuum is.

Grooming and Personal Care

Whatever you do to make yourself attractive goes under this category; it varies widely for different people. Gym memberships and supplements go here, as well as any accessories for the gym like clothes and gadgets. Hair salons, nail salons, body hair grooming, and similar services belong here as well. This category will also include products you buy like make up, shaving creams and utensils, and hair products. You might also like to put clothing purchases in here if they're not frequent or large. Clothing purchases should have their own category if you're spending more than 5% of your annual salary on them.

Medical

Somewhat of a niche category, but not a cheap one for those it applies to. If you have regular medication costs that are not covered by insurance, this is where they go. These can include contacts, glasses, birth control, pain medication, etc.

School and Office Supplies

People who are still in school and must spend a ton of money on textbooks and supplies are who this category is for. It can include small writing equipment like pens and paper, but also large ticket items like laptops and printers. If you're looking to replace a computer or buy computer equipment, this category can be quite large on an annual basis.

Alcohol and Other Activities

This is an offshoot of the entertainment category, but for some individuals it can be quite significant. Alcohol, cigarettes, and any recreational drugs that you indulge in are included in this category. Legality is irrelevant in this budgeting exercise. If you

spend more than 5% of your salary on something, it should get its own category.

Savings/Debt Repayment

This whole chapter is about this category! How much do you want to put away each month for non-consumption purposes? This can be any type of saving, including repaying debt, saving for a specific item like a vacation or a house, or long term savings for retirement. How you allocate this section is up to you. To calculate how much you will save each month, you deduct all your expense categories from your monthly income to see how much you have left over. If you're unhappy with this amount, you have to tweak the other categories or earn more income. No real way around that, unfortunately.

Now that you're familiar with how to categorize spending, you can pick a method for budgeting that will work with your personality and time constraints. But before we do that, let's analyze the spending of some example individuals.

Budgeting Stories

Throughout this section, I'll take you through the budgeting transitions of three individuals. Let's call them Lawrence, Lily, and Lamar. I've created a three month history of transactions for the three of them to show common spending patterns for people in their situations (according to my not so scientific research).

I've listed the detailed spending history of each person in the spreadsheets that accompany this book[22], and will summarize it here.

Let's meet our new friends.

Lawrence is 24 years old, six months into his first job at a large consulting firm.

Income: $60,000 a year.

Housing Situation: He lives with a roommate in a nice condominium in downtown Vancouver; they split all apartment related bills.

Transportation Situation: Lawrence drives a total of 20 km to his workplace every day in his leased two year old vehicle.

Entertainment: Lawrence enjoys the finer things in life, having a few drinks with friends at their favourite bar every weekend and indulges in other recreational substances every once in a while.

Food Spending: Lawrence's co-workers always go out for lunch, so he joins them every day and generally eats out on the weekends as well.

Grooming: He uses his company's perks to get a discounted gym membership and doesn't really care much for other grooming other than a haircut every other month.

Office Supplies: His laptop is old but he's not interested in replacing it for a few years, since he uses his company laptop for personal stuff as well.

Lawrence has no plans to marry, have kids, or buy a home at the moment. He likes living in his apartment downtown and he's happy to retire at the normal age of 65.

Pieced from credit card and bank account history, his last three months of spending look like this:

	Month 1	Month 2	Month 3
Income	$3,769.86	$3,769.86	$3,769.86
Expenses			
Housing	$1,217.25	$1,217.25	$1,217.25
Transportation	$993.41	$943.46	$878.46
Food - Groceries	$235.00	$255.00	$240.00
Food - Eating Out	$514.15	$434.96	$470.46
TV/Phone/Internet	$105.00	$105.00	$105.00
Entertainment	$189.41	$247.91	$167.91
Household Expenses	$30.00	$0.00	$20.00
Grooming and Personal Care	$0.00	$100.00	$450.00
Miscellaneous	$75.00	$200.00	$0.00
Savings	$410.64	$266.28	$220.78

After going through this exercise, Lawrence is happy he's saving money! Can he afford to continue with his budget this way? Is his retirement going to be okay?

Lily is 20 years old, in her second year of an engineering degree at a university in a large city.

Income: She works part-time during the school year to support herself and pay down her student debt. In the summers, she works full-time at an internship which she got through her school's career services.

Housing Situation: Lily lives in a room in a house off-campus, sharing the rent and other expenses with six other people.

Food Spending: She cooks most of her meals at home, but will indulge in going out to eat once a week or so.

Grooming: Lily uses the University's facilities to stay healthy, which are included in her tuition.

Office Supplies: Lily's parents gifted her a new laptop when she started school, so her office supplies expenses are limited to textbooks, paper, pens, and an expensive calculator.

Transportation: Lily does not own a car and uses public transportation every day.

Entertainment: Lily is an occasional smoker and drinks wine at home, going through a bottle of wine and two packs of cigarettes a week.

When she graduates, Lily will have a loan balance of $20,000 for her first two years of tuition, with $10,000 per year for the next two. The loan terms are 2.5% interest and interest starts six months after graduation. She also wants to buy a home in her area by age 30, and she's happy to retire at the normal retirement age of 65.

Her last three months of spending look like this:

	Month 1	Month 2	Month 3
Income	$1,777.38	$1,777.38	$1,777.38
Expenses			
Housing	$671.43	$671.43	$671.43
Transportation	$150.00	$150.00	$150.00
Food - Groceries	$300.00	$300.00	$300.00
Food- Eating Out	$159.00	$184.00	$184.00
TV/Phone/Internet	$84.29	$84.29	$84.29
Entertainment	$226.29	$266.00	$182.89
School Supplies	$25.00	$25.00	$600.00
Household Expenses	$15.00	$0.00	$15.00
Grooming and Personal Care	$15.00	$45.00	$0.00
Miscellaneous	$75.00	$100.00	$0.00
Savings	$56.37	-$48.34	-$410.23

Can she continue with her budget this way? Can she meet her goals? After checking all of her expenses over the last 3 months, Lily is not optimistic about her goals. We'll try to help her with that.

Lamar is 26 year old, 3 years into a career in marketing.

Income: $50,000 a year.

Housing Situation: He lives with a roommate in a nice condominium in downtown Toronto; they split all apartment related bills.

Food Spending: Food and personal grooming are Lamar's hobbies, he loves high quality food and looking good is very important to him. Lamar does not go out to eat for lunch with his coworkers because he brings his own home-cooked meals, but will go out to nice restaurants for dinner five times a week (including weekends).

Grooming: The gym is also important to Lamar; he goes to a popular venue and takes supplements to look his best. Monthly hair and nail salon appointments are a requirement for Lamar, as well as a new outfit once in a while.

Entertainment: Lamar does not drink alcohol or do any recreational drugs. He doesn't go out much either.

Office Supplies: Like Lawrence, his company provides him with a laptop that he uses.

Transportation: Lamar lives close to his work and only needs transportation a few times a week to other activities, which he uses public transit for.

Lamar wants to buy an apartment in a few years and has a long, international vacation planned for the year. He's happy to retire at the normal retirement age of 65 with an income below his own.

His last three months of spending look like this:

	Month 1	Month 2	Month 3
Income	$3,174.10	$3,174.10	$3,174.10
Expenses			
Housing	$1,166.50	$1,166.50	$1,166.50
Transportation	$30.00	$30.00	$30.00
Food - Groceries	$320.00	$470.00	$320.00
Food - Eating Out	$877.00	$877.00	$837.00
TV/Phone/Internet	$105.00	$105.00	$105.00
Entertainment	$36.50	$36.50	$36.50
Household expenses	$15.00	$0.00	$15.00
Grooming and Personal Care	$243.99	$203.99	$253.99
Miscellaneous	$0.00	$0.00	$0.00
Savings	$380.12	$285.12	$410.12

Lamar is very optimistic about his savings, no wonder he has $5,000 saved up! But will he be able to meet his lofty goals? An apartment in Toronto isn't cheap and he has to fund his one month pan-Asian vacation!

It's pretty clear that none of these individuals are fully aware of how their spending reflects on their ability to fulfill their goals. We'll go through their situations together and help them gradually lower their spending and create plans to make their dreams come true. But first, let's drop some knowledge.

Budgeting Methods
Envelope System
In this system, you divide all budgeted monthly expenses into separate envelopes. When you get paid, you withdraw the cash and divide it amongst the envelopes according to the amounts you've budgeted. That's it. That's all you get to spend in each category that month. If there's no money left over in a particular envelope, you have no more spending room in that category.

How strict you want to be with yourself is up to you, but the tougher you are the better this method works.

Pros
This method is very simple and easy to follow. You don't have to track individual expenses, which is a plus for some. The cash focus also makes spending tangible, allowing you to see every single dollar spent. Having to physically fork over cash for each transaction will make you think harder about what you're spending your money on, which will hopefully help you hone in on which purchases really makes you happy.

Cons
If you're interested in tracking, this method can make it hard to keep track of what you spent money on because you need to keep and organize receipts. The cash factor can also be frustrating to individuals that dislike using cash for day to day transactions and going to the bank on a regular basis.

If taken seriously, this system is highly restrictive. Once you've run out of cash in one envelope you must not spend in that category until the end of the month. Some personality types will be rubbed the wrong way by this and will be actively discouraged by this level of restriction. If you know that you can't be constrained this way, move along to a different system.

50/30/20 Rule

In this system, your spending is based on the percentages of after tax income that each expense uses up. This method dictates that spending should be split as follows:

50%–No more than 50% of after tax pay can be used on necessities. This usually includes rent, utilities, internet, transportation, and groceries.

20%–A minimum of 20% of after tax pay should be going to debt repayment or savings, but not short term savings like a vacation.

30%–No more than 30% of the cash you take home should be spent on non-essential lifestyle items like eating out, shopping, etc.

Pros

A 20% savings rate is double the conventional wisdom! If you can stick with this type of budgeting or just this rate of savings, you'll probably be just fine.

The specific percentages in this method would also allow you to reassess what you consider necessities. It can point out items in your spending that you might have misclassified in your everyday life. Common items that would probably prompt some questioning would be an expensive car or large home if you spend more than 50% of your take home pay in that category.

Cons

The percentages this method uses don't work for all life stages and lifestyle types. For example, students might have a much higher percentage than 50% for essentials due to a low or non-existent income. The key here would be to adjust the percentages depending on your situation.

This method also doesn't take into account the wide variety of incomes and how each category would be realistically affected. 50% of $50,000, $100,000, and $1,000,000 are very different numbers. Individuals who have these incomes probably don't spend two and fifty times more on necessities just because they make more. The more you make, the more you'll have to adjust the percentages in this method.

Digital Budgeting

This isn't so much a budgeting method as it is a tracking mechanism, but it's very popular, so we'll talk about it. The idea is that you open an account with an online budgeting app and connect your credit and bank accounts. Whenever a transaction comes through, the app or website will classify it for you. The app will keep track of all your spending categories and their totals. Some might even email you when you're close to a spending limit for the month.

The app will track and record all expenses and incomes for the month and allow you to create reports for yourself to see comparisons to your goals. Your only job with this method is to check the app and be thoughtful about how you spend money, along with a check-up every once in a while to make sure you're meeting your goals.

Pros

Once you've set up the accounts and classified initial transactions, it's so convenient! You might have to go back every so often to make sure the app counts transactions in the right categories, but otherwise everything is done for you.

The reports and email reminders are also a great tool to prompt you to think about your finances, make sure you enable those in the settings.

Cons

People who need more structure might find this method too easy to disregard and go back to their old spending ways.

Security will be a concern for some people who are unwilling to link their financial accounts with third party services. This is a common drawback of this method for many people, since some banks frown upon providing your passwords to outside parties.

Spreadsheet Budgeting

Exactly the same as digital budgeting, but you do it all yourself in a spreadsheet. It has a slightly different set of pros and cons than the digital method above though. I've provided a sample spreadsheet that I use to track my finances[23].

Pros

No security concerns; all the information in the spreadsheets is maintained in a safe place and access is restricted as you see fit.

Similar to cash transactions, having to physically enter each line of spending allows you to spend time reflecting on your spending and how you feel about a particular purchase. This can be useful in thinking about what's important to you and adjusting the budget accordingly.

Cons

If you have a lot of transactions, this is a very labour intensive way to keep track of them. This amount of work turns most people off from this method.

Reverse Budgeting

This method is interesting since it focuses on only one category, savings (or debt repayment, if you have debt). To use this method, you create an aggressive savings goal and that is the only target you try to hit every month. You can't resort to credit cards to pick up any spillover. It's a very niche method for those looking to save rather high percentages of their incomes without looking to really classify the rest.

Pros

If saving is the most important thing about budgeting to you, this laser-focused method could be good at helping you reach your goals.

Cons

This method doesn't really allow for focusing on spending habits and fixing them. According to this method, as long as savings goals are met, it doesn't matter how you got there.

Generally, the savings amount as a percentage of income is quite high, to a restrictive degree when it comes to all other spending.

Every one of these methods can be altered to align more with your particular goals and personality. You can also combine two methods to best suit your needs, like using the 50/30/20 method with digital budgeting. Picking a method that works for you and your lifestyle is very important. Budgets work best when they're not working against you.

A Note on Irregular Incomes

A lot of individuals in this world don't get paid a steady salary but are instead paid hourly, by commission, or some other variable form of income. These people might have difficulty using the above methods, since those budgets allocate all income to different functions without allowing for fluctuation in income. What if you make less than what the budget is based on, what gets eliminated? Instead of using the methods above, I would advise individuals that have irregular income to create a priority list of budget lines. As soon as you get paid, what is the most important expense that has to be paid? Rent, basic food, and transportation probably make up your top three. You can prioritize to spend on the rest of the items if you have enough income during that particular month. Make sure to include a savings item in whatever position you feel it deserves. Your priorities are your own.

Should You Set Up Automatic Bill Payments?

There is a way to set all your bills to automatically pay themselves, but should you do it? With today's technology you can have most of your financial life on autopilot.

There's a lot to love about automatic payments. They're super convenient since there's no need for five or more alerts in your calendar to pay bills. A big reason recently for using credit cards to pay for everything is getting those juicy rewards we discussed in the credit cards section. It's also more environmentally friendly, since you won't be getting bills to your home every month (if you set up paperless billing along with automatic payments). And on top of all of that, your credit score is also less likely to take a hit since you'll never forget a payment!

On the other hand, there are also potential downsides to using an automated system. You're probably going to stop checking your bills, or at least check them less often, now that you can pay them automatically. This can lead to overspending and unnoticed errors. If you have any items coming out of your bank account directly, you could also potentially be hit with insufficient funds (NSF) fees from the bank if you didn't have enough money in the account to make the payment.

If you think you can mitigate the negatives, automating bill payments is awesome. In order to set this up, you can go to the websites of the vendors you use, like the phone or internet companies. They will generally allow you to create automatic payments linked to a credit card. After you've done that, you'll have a monthly credit card total. Now, set up a bill in your bank account for that total to go from your bank account to the credit card in order to pay the balance off in full. If you use the card for non-automated expenses, you'll have to top up the payment when the bill is due, but automatic billing takes a lot of the hassle out of paying bills each month.

Budgeting Aides

Mint

Mint is probably the most well-known budget helper around. It's a website and mobile application where you link all your bank accounts and credit card accounts and the website will then keep track of and catalogue all the transactions for you. You can set monthly goals, which are displayed on the home page with your progress towards them. Mint would fall under the Digital Budgeting method.

The website is user friendly and pleasing to the eye, with a clean and simple interface. Setup can take less than five minutes since most large banks are compatible with Mint's systems. Once you input all your accounts and their passwords, Mint will go in and download the transactions.

Once all transactions are downloaded, Mint will assign vendor names and categories to each one (an example would be a pizza vendor being classified under Fast Food). With this information, Mint will also create monthly spending graphs based on their categories. This can pretty eye opening for people who have never budgeted before.

You can manually add cash based transactions and, which allows you to see your full financial situation.

Within the website, you can set monthly goals for budget categories, set reminders and alerts for bills, and set alerts for warnings when spending gets too close to the category total.

Pros

- Quick setup and the site is easy to use and aesthetically pleasing
- Graphs and charts are useful, attractive, and the ability to set up alerts is very convenient
- Mint has great financial goal integration for goal setting and tracking
- Free!
- Mint is not only a budgeting software; it also helps you keep track of your investments and net worth

Cons

- Categorization of expenses could use some work. Many individuals will find the need to take some time to re-categorize expenses into the right buckets
- It can be hard to link up investment accounts because Mint doesn't support all financial institutions and vice versa
- Two-factor authentication on other accounts might pose a problem with getting Mint into your accounts
- Advertising for other services is fairly prevalent. If this bothers you, Mint will be a no go
- Security will be a concern for some people who are unwilling to link their financial accounts with third party services. Some banks will cancel purchase protection if you're a Mint user, since you did willingly give away your password

You Need a Budget (YNAB)

YNAB is a good example of a product that only does one thing, but does it well. Hardcore budgeters love it for this reason. It's a budgeting application that's similar to Mint, but the approach it takes is very different.

The app guides you through assigning every dollar of your paycheque to some category, be it spending or savings. Common categories are provided so you don't have to create new ones for obvious things. Creating and customizing new categories is easy. As the month goes on and transactions come in, the goal is to spend as close to your goals in each category as possible.

Pros

- Tutorials and learning tools are key for beginners and provide a good guide to the software, as well as introducing various budgeting concepts
- There is less 'set it and forget it' automation with YNAB, which makes you pay more attention to your money and habits

Cons

- YNAB costs $5 per month or $50 per year to use
- Categorization is not automatic, meaning you'll have to log in every now and then to categorize all your spending
- At the time of writing, the security authentication processes are a little less high tech than Mint's
- Some functionality is lacking, like transferring money in between accounts

There are other budgeting apps and software like Every Dollar and Quicken, but I find that most people won't go further in their search of budgeting help than Mint or YNAB. Both have huge followings and are the go-to budget apps.

Reduction Techniques

Once you've gone over your previous spending and made some saving and financial goals, it's time to reduce the budget or increase income in order to meet them. Increasing income is a very personal matter, which may or may not be possible depending on your current employment situation and lifestyle, so we won't talk about that here. Expense reduction is the next step if you can't increase income. We'll approach expense reduction on a few levels, since intensities vary.

Let's look at reducing expenses in our main categories on four difficulty settings: easy, medium, hard, and extreme.

Housing

Housing is usually a large percentage of anybody's monthly spending. However, due to the nature of this category it's generally hard to reduce it significantly.

Housing's main attributes are size, location, and privacy. Take a look at your current living arrangements and think about which of these characteristics is the most important to you in a living situation. The ability to reduce items in any category will be based on your degree of interest in each of the attributes of a particular category.

Easy

The fastest and least painful way to reduce housing expenses is to call your insurance company and try to negotiate a lower rate. However, even if you're successful, the amount of savings will be miniscule compared to a rent or mortgage payment.

In order to get big savings out of your insurance company, you might have to change the deductible on your plan. A deductible is the amount you'll pay out of pocket before the insurance company covers anything. Raising the deductible works to reduce insurance costs in two ways: by reducing your premiums, and reducing renewal costs if you have a claim. Smaller deductibles create claims any time an insurable event occurs, which drives up your premiums. A higher deductible creates fewer claims since you'll pay out of pocket for small losses. The more the insurance company has to cover, the higher the premiums as well. In order to figure out what a good deductible would be, you need to do a break-even analysis comparing any higher outlay in case of an insurable event to the decrease in premiums. This is a much bigger deal for homeowner's insurance than renter's insurance.

Medium

Slightly more hassle comes out of reducing utilities costs. For most people, that means paying close attention to timing activities (if your rates change depending on the times of the day like mine do), or actively doing less utility related activities, like running the dishwasher less often. Other utility reducing activities are taking shorter showers and turning off lights when not in use.

Hard

The next thing you can do is move to a cheaper place. Before you take this option, keep in mind that the expenses and headaches associated with moving should be taken into account before you take the plunge. The difference in cost on the home should exceed the moving costs, and then provide the savings you were looking for on top of that.

If you own a home, you can try refinancing the mortgage at a lower rate, or decreasing the timeline of your payments. Refinancing is only worth it if the savings equal 1% or more of the interest rate due to the associated refinancing costs. Shortening your mortgage period from 30 to 20 or even 15 years will save a ton on interest payments, but also increase the monthly payment. Make sure that you can handle the increase if you're interested in this option.

Extreme

The next three options will be difficult for many, but if you need the room in your budget it could work out for you. The first is renting a basement apartment, which may be a cheaper than a regular apartment, but less desirable for a lot of people. Next is moving into a room in a house where several people rent out a whole house and share living space. This is common in student housing and can be half the price of a one bedroom apartment. Giving up a bit of privacy can be worth it. The last is moving back to your parents' house. If that's an option for you, and you won't be miserable doing it, this is generally the cheapest option.

Transportation

Transportation comes in three types: personal (your own car), public, and private (cabs). For young people, this category can get very expensive, due to higher insurance rates and lease payments.

The characteristics that you might value for transportation are speed, reliability, and convenience. Take a look at what you use currently for transportation outside of getting to work. What characteristic drew you to your current transportation situation? What are you willing to give up?

Easy

The easiest way to reduce transportation costs if you have a vehicle is to shop around for insurance and be very thorough about it. Insurance rates vary widely across different companies.

You could also keep an eye out for gas price changes and fill up when prices are at their lowest, reducing your average price of gas.

If you're currently leasing a car, it would be a good idea to see if you can buy it instead. A loan might be necessary, but it would still be cheaper than leasing. Leasing is the highest moneymaker for car dealerships, auto loans a somewhat distant second. If you must own a car and can't buy it for cash, at least get a loan instead of leasing.

Medium

The next rung of difficulty goes to buying an older vehicle. This is harder in two ways: it takes more time to save up to buy the car, and you have to pay more attention to maintenance issues. While you may spend more money on maintenance, an older car will generally cost less overall than a more recent model. Used cars also factor in depreciation much better than newer cars, so you get a better deal when buying. 63% of the original value of a car is wiped out in the first five years of the car's existence[24].

Hard
Ditch the car entirely in favour of public transport! This will be extremely difficult for some people since distances and access to public transport vary widely around this country. Public transport is much cheaper than vehicle ownership in most cases, even if you have to use multiple transit systems. What you sacrifice with public transit is speed and the ability to customize your route, but at least you gain some free time to read books like this one.

Extreme
What's even more extreme than public transit, you ask? Biking. Even fewer people will be able to ride a bicycle everywhere due to distances from their home to work, but for those who live within 10km and are reasonably healthy, it's definitely possible. And you're exercising too, so it's a double benefit. Cycling only costs as much as your initial bicycle does, plus annual maintenance. It's by far the cheapest transport method, but also the toughest.

Food
This is where most of us spend the lion's share of non-essential spending. Eating out is an extremely popular pastime with the younger generation, and it shows in our spending. When it comes to eating food that we don't cook, we value the following: convenience, taste, and health. Take a look at your spending history, which we discussed in the tracking section, and see which characteristics your food purchases follow. What do you really value when you eat out?

Easy

The fastest things you can eliminate are the purchases that don't add value, the food you buy without thinking which doesn't make you particularly happy. For most people, these would be coffee in the morning, last minute impulse snacks at the grocery store, and the 'I'm too tired to cook' dinner you grab on the way home that's neither delicious, nor healthy.

Next up are small reductions in consumption when you go out to eat. Instead of ordering alcohol or drinks with meals, asking for water will lower your bill by a few dollars. Another thing that will reduce the bill further is not ordering appetizers at a restaurant.

Medium

To get to this level, you're going to want to start dropping restaurant meals. Instead of going out five times a week, maybe go down to three or two. Whatever works with your budget and goals. Cooking more meals at home will almost always reduce overall food expenses, unless you're a gourmet cook that buys very fancy ingredients.

Another way to reduce the grocery bill is to buy store brand foods instead of name brand items. Metro's soup brand instead of Campbell's, for example. This practice can take off a bit off the top of your receipt.

Hard

To save even more money, you'll have to cook a majority of your meals at home, with the exception of a few special occasions. Initially, it'll be hard to refuse lunches with coworkers, but you'll notice that you'll be healthier and your wallet will thank you too. As you learn new recipes and get in the groove of preparing meals ahead of time, it will get easier.

This level also requires you to buy less processed foods and shop at discount retailers if they are available in your area. Grocery stores change their pricing according to area, so don't be afraid to try different grocers to see where you can get the best deals.

Extreme

What can be harder than cooking almost all your meals at home?
Being vegetarian while doing it. Meat is a very big part of the
common North American diet, and it doesn't come cheap. Other
sources of protein can be much lighter on your wallet, like eggs
and legumes.

While it can be tempting to live off $0.33 ramen noodle
packages and rice and beans to pay off your student loans faster,
don't ruin your health if you can afford to eat better.

Entertainment

Entertainment is easily the most subjective category. It can mean
so many different things to different people. Some people will
classify alcohol and clubbing expenses as entertainment. For
others, it'll be tickets to events like concerts and museums. For
others still, it'll be the costs of video games or board games. Due to
the variety of this particular category, it doesn't make sense to lay
out each level of difficulty for each type of person. The best thing
to do is list all your entertainment expenses from most happiness
producing to least and eliminate accordingly. Don't buy things
that don't make you happy!

Examples Revisited

Let's go back to our friends and see how we can help them, now that we've looked at budgeting methods and ways to reduce your budget in order to meet your goals.

Lawrence

If Lawrence wants to continue having the same level of income he has now in retirement, he needs to have $2,396,791 when he's 65 (assuming a 6% return after inflation and a 92-year lifespan)[25]. In order to get to that amount of money by 65 he should be putting away $771 on a monthly basis! That's a shocking 15.4% of his income. His current average monthly savings of $300 will get him to $932,603 by 65. Right off the bat, Lawrence finds both the average monthly savings needed to reach his goal, and his current projected retirement savings unacceptable. To make the situation better, he decided to reduce his retirement spending to $50,000 a year, which means he'll now need $1,997,430, reducing his monthly savings needs to $643.

Lawrence predicts that his income will go up to $80,000 in the next 5 years, so he wants to offset some of the retirement savings to his later years. He feels he can't reduce his budget that far at his current level of salary, plus he needs to have a vacation too! He wants to go to Japan this year and it'll cost around $3,500 for a two-week trip. To save up for that he needs to put aside $292 per month. That's almost his entire savings used up for a vacation. Pushing retirement savings as far back as possible and prioritizing short term indulgences is fairly common these days, but remember that this has its consequences!

We're going to look at this in two ways: one where we let Lawrence have his way and only save partially for retirement now and save more later, and one where we'll prioritize retirement now.

Lawrence prioritized his expenses in the following way according to happiness they give him:

1. Lunch with coworkers–networking opportunity to increase his earning potential, plus yummy food

2. Apartment
3. Drinks with friends
4. Weekend meals with friends
5. Movies
6. Christmas gifts
7. Car expenses–only method of transport available
8. Recreational drugs–alleviate the stress of work
9. Household expenses–unavoidable
10. Breakfast and coffees–mainly a convenience

Scenario One: Vacation First, and Some Retirement Savings
The first thing to do is to set financial goals. Let's arbitrarily say that he should save the vacation fund and an additional $500 towards retirement every month. That's a total of $800 per month in savings, around a 20% savings rate. Lawrence does not believe in needing an emergency fund since his work is very stable, and his car is unlikely to need work because it's new and he treats it well.

To make it a gradual transition, we're going to reduce his spending in waves. Cold turkey approaches don't work for everyone, and Lawrence believes he's the kind of person that needs a gradual change.

The first wave of reductions will come from the last rung of the happiness scale, the breakfasts and coffee each work day. This will only reduce his average monthly expenses by $56, or 1.6%, because we would need to add some money towards groceries to make coffee and breakfast at home. We're looking to cut anywhere from 5% to 20% the first go around, so let's look for more stuff to cut.

Since the essential expenses portion of Lawrence's spending is so high let's look at that. This amount is made up largely of home and car expenses. Lawrence's home is his second priority, so we'll leave it alone. What about the car? He uses it to drive to work which is 10km away. A similar taxi ride would cost $18 each way, and would add up to $720 per month. This is a significant decrease in spending and will take away any surprise maintenance costs. Alternatively, Lawrence has a co-worker that lives in his area who's willing to carpool with him for gas costs of $100 per week. Given that this will save him half his transportation expenses and provide prime networking time, Lawrence wants to choose this option. He'll have to supplement with some cab rides for going out, but since he lives downtown he thinks he can keep this cost under $50 per month. But what about the lease he's still on the hook for? In this scenario, we'll pretend Lawrence found a person who will take over his lease with no problems and he'll only have to pay $300 to transfer the lease. Leases are a nightmare to get rid of in real life, so this is not realistic.

That brings us to a reduction of $754 on average, about a 13% decrease in total expenses. Not bad for only eliminating two things! Not quite our $800 per month savings goal yet, but baby steps. Lawrence will try to keep to this budget for a month or so, and then we can reassess if we cut the right expenses and where we can cut more.

Once Lawrence is sure he can keep up this budget up, we're going to cut a bit deeper. His drug use is his third least-favourite expense, and it's not a small one. If he can find a way to moderate stress from his job without this expense, he can bring his savings total up to $810 per month.

But we know $810 is not enough monthly savings for his long term goals. If he keeps this savings rate up, he will need to contribute about $100 more every month when he starts getting paid more.

$100 might not sound like a huge difference, but what if during those five years he meets the love of his life and they want to get married and buy a house? Retirement savings will probably go out the window, putting him further away from his goals. If his wedding and home down payment savings take him an additional five years (with the help of his partner), he'll now be 29 and will have to save $200 more to make up the savings difference, on top of his mortgage payment and other expenses.

Scenario Two: Mega Saver Mode, Both Vacation and Retirement
What if Lawrence buckled down and started saving for retirement as well as his vacation? To do both, he would need to save $935

every month. That's a massive portion of his income, but very possible.

The majority of this savings can be made with one change, and again it'll be Lawrence's transportation expenses. What if he took public transit for $150 per month? He'd save an average of $988, which is a 20% decrease in expenses per month. This is a big change, so we'll let Lawrence live with it for a month or so and see how he adapts.

Turns out he loves it since he can get work done or listen to podcasts on the bus. That gets him to his goal, but Lawrence is a little wary of the potential partner and house that could be in his future. He wants to save a little more just in case. Let's take out those coffees and recreational drugs again, since he was fine with those changes in the previous scenario. This leaves us with an average monthly savings of $1,124! Lawrence is happy with that and wants to call it a day.

Let's see how this new savings amount affects his future situation. If he stopped contributing again because of the wedding and housing costs, what would his monthly retirement savings need to be? If it takes four years instead of five years to save up for the wedding and down payment with this higher savings rate, he'll start contributing again at 28. He would need to put in about $200 less! $200 per month in extra spending money is not a bad deal.

Lily

Lily's situation is very different from Lawrence's. She's younger and her priority is her debt, which will be $40,000 when she graduates in 2 years. She also wants to buy a $350,000 house in 10 years with a down payment of $70,000. Lily expects her salary out of university to be similar to Lawrence's for the first 5 years.

At her current spending, Lily could get rid of her debt about 14 months out of university, including the interest. The debt repayment timeline includes her current monthly savings amount of $590, and her future monthly savings of $1,916. She can then focus these monthly savings into her down payment which she'll reach 37 months later, when she's 27.

This seems very promising. She can even keep her bad habits like smoking and still be okay financially. But smoking kills, so she should stop.

This is the power of working throughout university, nabbing a great summer job, and maintaining a student lifestyle even through adulthood. This situation may not be available to all types of students, but it can help start your working life without debt and get you ready to conquer your goals. It's possible that Lily won't fully stick to her old lifestyle once she starts work, but her savings rate is still in a great place for her goals.

What about retirement? If Lily wants $50,000 as her retirement income, she'll need to have $1,922,021 when she's 65 (assuming a 6% return after inflation and a 92-year lifespan)[26]. In order to get to that amount of money by 65 she should be putting away $519 on a monthly basis. Lily's first and second priorities are her loans and house. What if she starts to save for retirement after the down payment is paid for? To get to $1,922,021 if she started saving at 27, Lily would need to put in $714. Her future monthly savings is $1,916 per month, so it seems like she'll be able to swing it.

Lamar

Lamar is happy with living on $40,000 in retirement, which is lower than his current income. To do that, he needs to have $1,355,201 when he's 65 (assuming a 6% return and a 92-year lifespan). In order to get to that amount of money by 65, he should be putting away $513 on a monthly basis. That's about 12.3% of his income. His current average of $358 in savings per month will get him to $946,477. But that ignores the down payment on the apartment that he wants to buy in 3 years. His down payment will be about $60,000 ($300,000 apartment), so he'll need to save $1,667 per month. Lamar's $5,000 month-long vacation will add another $417 to his monthly required savings. Obviously, it will be impossible for Lamar to meet all these goals on his current salary and current spending level, the savings would take up 82% of his current monthly income.

Lamar doesn't expect his income to increase much over his career, so he can either alter his spending or pick up a part-time job, or both. Lamar doesn't want to delay his retirement savings further, since he has seen his parents struggling with this problem. He is willing to make sacrifices and forego vacations for 3 years in order to get his apartment. Lamar is still set on buying the apartment in three years, so he'll need to save $2,180 each month to get there. He is very committed to his goals and wants to give it his best effort.

Lamar prioritized his expenses in the following way according to happiness:
1. Eating out with friends
2. Gym membership and supplements
3. Cooking meals at home
4. Clothing
5. Nail appointments
6. Apartment
7. Netflix

Savings goals as large as those Lamar is working towards will take several iterations of a budget to accomplish, since we don't want to be too drastic all at once. Lamar will also want to look at additional work to make his goals a reality.

Lamar doesn't put a lot of stock in his apartment, so he might be able to move somewhere cheaper. If he's not set on apartment living, he can look for a living situation similar to Lily's for the three years till he gets his apartment, which will save him $495 every month. I don't know a person who's not addicted to Netflix but if he doesn't love it, he can remove that too. These two changes bring his savings up to an average of $884 per month, a 19% reduction from his earlier expenses.

Since Lamar is very close with a lot of restaurant owners, he was able to get himself a waiter position at one of his favourite spots. It'll bring in about $1,000 per month after taxes and he will get a free meal per shift. Lamar will have to give up one of his weekend days to do this, but the rest of the shifts work around his existing schedule. This only reduces his spending by an additional 3%, but hugely impacts his savings which are up to $1,953 per month. Can Lamar find an extra $227 in his budget for the rest of his savings goal? He's starting to feel stretched.

It's time to look for less painful ways to reduce his expenses. Is $70 the absolute best deal he can get on his cell phone plan? Would he be willing to go to a slightly cheaper gym? Would he be willing to skip his nail appointments and paint them himself at home? Lamar knows of a cheaper phone provider that only charges $35 a month, and their reception is good in his area. He's willing to go to a gym that charges $40 per month instead of $50, but he won't compromise on the nail appointments. This leaves him with monthly savings of $1,998. It's a bit lower than he'd hoped, but his lifestyle makes him far too happy to exchange it for a few hundred dollars of retirement money. Lamar pledges that he'll make it up after his down payment is saved. He might pick up an extra shift at the restaurant as well, if it really comes down to it.

The examples above are the stories of three very different people with different goals and different attitudes towards savings. I've ignored investing here because it'll be discussed in the next part of the book. But I wanted to show you that budgeting and saving money is not a one size fits all approach and that saving doesn't mean cutting out the things that make you truly happy.

Buying Guide

Buying stuff we don't needs makes us humans incredible happy in the short term. That's why shopaholics exist! It's even worse with an expensive item, we get such a rush from it that our body responds to it very strongly. Increased heart rate, sweating, an explosion of endorphins, and adrenaline engulfs us. No wonder Black Friday is such a horrorshow.

Clearly, we're not rational beings when it comes to being faced with a large purchasing decision, so what can you do to make the process less primal and more logical?

1. Set a cool down period for yourself. Okay, so you want a catmobile (the bat one is copyrighted, unfortunately). You're at the dealership in the heat of the moment and you just WANT IT NOW. What if you wait a day? A month? Will you still want it and be willing to pay for it? Choose a time period that's far enough away for cooling down sufficiently. Use it to consider why you want the item and whether you agree with your own motives. You might believe the item will make you happy, fill whatever voids you have, or will grant you social acceptance, all of which are debatable and most likely won't happen. You need to give it one day at the minimum, but a week is better. Believe me, it'll probably still be there if you decide you still want it. If it isn't, you can console yourself with a cookie and count your money.

2. Understand what you're giving up by buying the item. What could that $50,000 that you would've spent on the catmobile (what a bargain!) get you if you don't spend it? Maybe it could buy you a year and a half's worth of rent. Maybe it would be worth millions of dollars if you invested it for 50 years. Maybe you can get three jet skis instead. Would you still prefer to buy the catmobile? Those thoughts are the first ones that come to mind when you regret a purchase, so it's best to pre-empt them.

3. If you know exactly what you want, maybe someone else has already bought it, got bored of it, and will sell it to you? It's great because the item will be barely used and the depreciation on the full purchase price is already accounted

for. Buying used means the seller is rarely motivated by profit, they probably just want it out of their house, so they might even throw in free accessories!

4. If you've decided to get the item new, you should negotiate to make sure you get the best deal on it. You might not be able to negotiate with Costco or Wal-Mart, but you can definitely bring the price of a car or a house down. Even furniture stores will negotiate with you! It literally never hurts to ask. Oh, and bring cash. Nothing says 'I mean business and I'm ready to buy' like a stack of hundies. Sales people will fawn over you. If they still don't come down to a reasonable amount, turn around and walk away. There are other vendors that will want your business. They want that cash!

   Don't be afraid to show indifference to whatever you're buying too. Being excited and giddy about something only makes the salesperson's life easier, since they know you want it. Be quiet and say as little as possible. Disagree as much as possible without being rude.

That's pretty much it, good luck with your next big purchase!

3 Investing

Investing: Why it Matters

Investing...the word that strikes more fear into young people than 'commitment'. Shudder.

Too freaking bad. We're going to talk about it anyway, since it's very important for your future. Everybody has different opinions on investing and the best way to do it. I'm going to give you some examples of different ways people in certain positions can invest later on, but what I really want to do is prepare you to think for yourself when it comes to investing.

Why should you care about investing? Because investing is the fastest way to become rich without winning the lottery or starting a successful business (neither of which is statistically likely to happen to you[27]). Having your money in a savings account will earn little compared to the different options we'll discuss here due to something called inflation risk. What that means is that every year, your dollar loses value due to something called inflation. If you keep your money in a savings account, it's unlikely that any interest the account pays you will outstrip inflation, which is usually 2-3% a year usually. This means that over time you'll end up with less money that you started with.

Compound Interest makes this even worse. Let's say you have $1,000 to save every year and two options: A savings account that pays you 2% interest and the stock market which returns 5%. If you only invest for one year, the 3% difference doesn't seem like much, it's the difference between $20 and $50. Over time, this difference gets monstrous. In 25 years at the same situation, the savings account will be worth $34,312 and the stock market account $53,500[28]. That's almost 20 grand from a measly 3% difference in returns.

So how we get those types of growth percentages every year? You invest your money, and not just in a savings account.

What is Investing?

So, you get it now and you're hungry to put your money to work. Awesome. But first, let's back up a bit to understand what investing really is before throwing your money at it.

Investing is spending money on something with the expectation that you'll receive more in return than what you put in. This is called a return on investment. In this limited definition, investing can apply to many things. Putting yourself through education that you know will result in a better paying job, starting a business, or putting money into the 'market'. All of these are technically investments. We've already talked about education so let's focus on 'market' investing.

What is this mysterious 'market' I keep referring to? I'm referring to any place where you can trade investment instruments. Investment instruments are things like stocks and bonds that we'll define in detail later.

Almost all large countries have a stock market. Canada's main one is the Toronto Stock Exchange (TSX), where you'll find, for sale, parts of all Canadian companies that sell their ownership to the general public (more on this later). But down to its essence, what is a stock market?

A stock market is a marketplace where companies put up little pieces of themselves for the general public to buy. Once the company sells them, these 'shares' can be bought and sold by individuals as many times as they'd like amongst themselves. This buying and selling activity will move the price of that share up or down, depending on whether people want to own it or sell. Easy peasy.

To be able to 'trade' on a stock market, that is to buy and sell these mythical shares, you need to have an account at something called a brokerage. You can't just go up to the TSX building on Bay Street in Toronto and hand the receptionist $1,000 in cash and say 'Give me shares of X'. Brokerages exist within your bank, or as independent entities, where you move your money to buy and sell in that separate account. We'll talk about choosing a brokerage later on.

Another thing you should know about before buying things is that it costs you money to buy and sell shares through a brokerage. Every transaction can cost between $0-10 depending on the brokerage you choose and should be factored into all the math that surrounds investing. Yes, there will be math, calm down. Every time you want to buy or sell some shares, you will pay $0-10 on top of that. We'll touch on this later too.

As you can probably already tell, investing is kinda complicated at the beginning. Once you wrap your head around it, it won't be.

How Much Cash to Invest?

You have a general understanding of what a stock market is now. But how much of your savings should you put in there?

The key to investing successfully, for most people, is a long time horizon due to the powers of compound interest. However, most people have things in the short term that they want to set aside money for before they focus on retirement investing.

What Counts as Short Term or Long Term

Short term money should be anything you want to save up for in the next five years or so. Know you'll need a down payment on a home? Know that you'll be moving to a more expensive area? These are short term things you need to plan and save for, so keep that money outside of risky investments.

Should I Worry About Recessions?

If you think recessions and depressions are these terrifying once in a lifetime events, you're not alone. But this is simply not true, they happen all the time. The U.S. economy has experienced 23 recessions and depressions since 1900[29]. A recession is "a significant decline in economic activity spread across the economy, lasting more than two quarters, which is six months, normally visible in real gross domestic product (GDP), real income, employment, industrial production, and wholesale-retail sales"[30]. Basically, this is a period where it'll be hard to find work, you might be paid less if you have a job, and your stocks will tank. Not fun at all.

Despite many economists and finance types trying to predict the next recession or depression, they're notoriously difficult to anticipate accurately. Even though you might not be able to know when the next one is coming, you can definitely prepare for it.

The key to getting through a recession is having the money you actually need on hand instead of invested, because having money that you need losing its value during these times is terrifying. You don't want that $50,000 that you needed for your house's down payment falling from $50,000 to $35,101, which is what would have happened if you had $50,000 in the S&P Composite Index on September 19th, 2008, and then looked at your investments on October 10th, 2008, after it suffered a 29.8% drop in 20 days[31].

S&P TSX Composite Index in 2008/2009

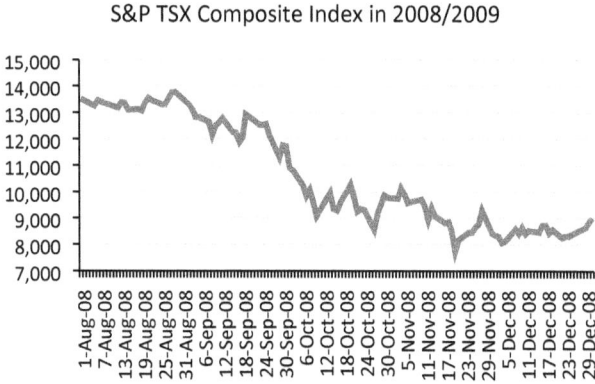

[32]

To avoid these situations, keep short term money where it will be safe from significant swings in value. We'll talk about emotions and investing later on in this section and how to mitigate the stress and fear associated with investing.

Goals

So what are your goals?

Most short term goals fall into the following categories:

- Paying down debt
- Education
- Buying a parakeet fluent in seven languages
- Housing down payment
- Large purchases (Furniture, appliances, home repairs, etc.)
- Car down payment

Okay, so maybe a multilingual parakeet isn't the best example of a short term goal, but a car down payment or paying off a line of credit definitely is. The money you save up for these items shouldn't be invested like the rest of your finances. We'll talk about riskiness in investing in a second, but what you need to know for now is that these amounts should only go in the low risk investments pile, since I'm sure you don't want them to drop in value when you need them

How Low Can You Go?

Risk Profile Assessment

Now that you know how much of your money you can invest in longer term pursuits, we need to figure out how to invest it. Figuring out what level of riskiness you can handle is the first step.

The way to do that is to consider your time horizon for these investments, and how willing you are to endure temporary losses for larger gains.

The easiest thing to figure out is your time horizon. When will you need to use this money that you're investing? I'm hoping the answer is 30-60 years. That's how long you should be saving and investing for retirement. Incidentally, this allows you to have a very open approach to risk because you have time on your side for the investments to grow.

The following questions will help you figure out where you land on the risk profile spectrum:

When do you plan on taking money out of your investments?

| 0-5 Years | 5-10 Years | 10-15 Years | 15-25 Years | 25-35 Years | 35-45 Years |

If you were invested in the market in 2008 when that 29.8% drop happened, what would you have done?

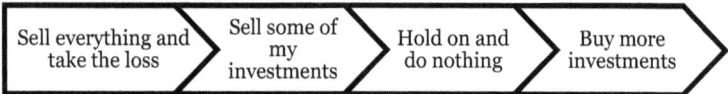

| Sell everything and take the loss | Sell some of my investments | Hold on and do nothing | Buy more investments |

Do you prefer investments whose values don't move much and are willing to take the lower reward? Or do you accept that big rewards come to those who are willing to accept large changes in value?

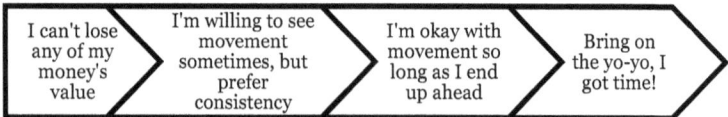

| I can't lose any of my money's value | I'm willing to see movement sometimes, but prefer consistency | I'm okay with movement so long as I end up ahead | Bring on the yo-yo, I got time! |

What is your income situation both currently and in the future?

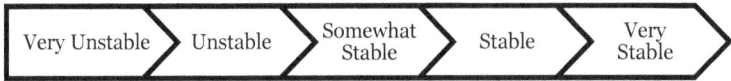

Very Unstable	Unstable	Somewhat Stable	Stable	Very Stable

Very unstable – I don't know where my next dollar will comes from

Unstable – my job might not be here for me in a year or two

Somewhat stable – I'll be able to keep a job for at least 3 years

Stable – I'm not getting fired any time soon

Very stable – my field is always hiring and I have great job security

The questions above are just an introduction for you to get a sense of how comfortable you might be with different types of investments. There are many great full length questionnaires out there on the internet that will give you a much more detailed idea of your risk profile.

Investing Mindsets

Aggressive

'Go big or go home' represents this mindset quite well. These are the people that need to make as much money as possible from their investments and won't accept low returns. Aggressive mindsets are towards the far right side of the questionnaire you just answered. Generally this type of investor will have a majority of their investments in so called 'risky' investments, with only a few less risky ones to balance things out.

Balanced

The Goldilocks approach: not too much risk, but not too much reward either. Happy to be somewhere in the middle, balanced investors don't chase big risky propositions for the extra couple percent of gains. These are the people towards the middle of the answers above. This approach's investments are split with the risky and non-risky investments closer towards having equal weight.

Risk Averse

These people are super afraid of losing any of their money. Keeping money in a bank account with a 2% interest sounds great to them, free money! Risk averse individuals care more about preserving what they have, instead of making fat stacks. This mindset corresponds with the far left of the graphs above. A majority of this type of investor's money will be invested in less risky investments.

Figuring out your risk appetite and time horizon before you start investing allows you to reduce the feeling of being overwhelmed by choice and decisions that many people experience when faced with the investing world. Let's look at some more concepts that will help reduce this feeling.

Diversification

This is one of the big buzzwords in investing. Everybody always talks about how 'diversified' their 'portfolio' is. The easiest and simplest way to explain this concept is to not 'put all your eggs in one basket', the fear being that something would happen to the basket. This is an old and clichéd saying, but damn is it effective. In adult language, it means having enough different investments that if one goes bankrupt or loses a lot of value, the whole is still okay and the losses are offset by potential gains in your other investments. Let's look at two quick examples to illustrate this.

In the first scenario, you own only one investment, stock of a particular company that depends on a strong economy to be profitable, something like a high-end car manufacturer. Let's say you have $500,000 invested in that company. One day, the economy decides that it's going to perform badly for a few years and as a result the value of your shares goes down to $300,000. Bummer.

What if you have two investments, the car company stock and the stock of a discount grocery chain. You still have $500,000 invested, but with half in each stock. When the market goes down, the car stock's value will still go down to $150,000. However, stock of the discount grocery chain will most likely go up since in a bad economic time people are more likely to go there than their usual grocery store. Let's say that stock goes up by 20% to $300,000. Your total investment is now worth $450,000 instead of $300,000. Diversification at work!

Now of course diversification can also mean the type of investments you hold, but we'll talk about that later.

Liquidity

Like the various states of matter (solids, liquids, and gasses), investments have different levels of something called liquidity. This trait measures how easy it is to transform cash into the investment and vice versa. If it's easy to do so, and can be done by any individual online or in person, then it's considered liquid. If you need help from someone else, or there are restrictions on the timing of buying or selling, it can be considered illiquid.

Why does this matter? Investments are places where you hold your money. Occasionally, you'll need to take that money out for whatever reason. Maybe you found a better deal somewhere else or you need the money for an emergency or your planned retirement withdrawals. Liquidity is what makes these changes possible.

Suppose a great investment opportunity to buy a rental property came up for you, but the developer was selling out quickly. How fast you can get your money out of one investment into another is its measure of liquidity. A stock can be sold for cash in an instant and the cash transferred to your bank account in a few days, a house could take months to sell.

Asset Allocations

More buzzwords! Investing is full of them, it's ridiculous. 'Assets' is another word for investments. 'Allocation' is simply how much of each type of investment you have. This concept is important because it goes hand in hand with the risk profile we've discussed before. Your risk profile dictates how you allocate your investments. Individuals with a more risky profile will have more risky investments and less non-risky investments. Vice versa for less risky investment profiles. We'll see this in some examples soon.

Portfolio Optimization

Portfolio is a fancy word for 'all the investments you hold' and 'optimization' means 'making something as awesome as possible', together they mean making the investments you hold as awesome and as close to your idea of perfect as humanly possible. But how do you achieve this? With the aforementioned asset allocation and something called rebalancing.

When you first start investing, you'll find out your risk profile and start investing according to the asset allocations that your personal risk profile dictates, using the investment types we'll discuss in a bit. This allocation is how much of each type of investment you want in your portfolio to match the exact amount of risk you want. Some people love stocks and hate bonds, some want real estate. Your asset allocation will need to match your investing personality.

As time goes on, some investments will go up in value and some will lose value. Rebalancing is the act of buying or selling investments to bring your allocations back into the original condition. It's a surefire and emotionless way to buy low and sell high, the hallmarks of good investing behaviour. How often this is done is up to you and depends entirely on your investment style. What's that? Glad you asked!

What's Your Style?

People who invest generally come in two flavours, active investors and passive investors. The names are pretty self-explanatory but I'll break it down with examples to make sure it makes sense.

Active Investors

These are the people who live and breathe investing. They work on their portfolios with the goal to be better than the general market, making as much money as possible through frequent buying and selling of investments. The main motivator for active investors is profit, and they're generally much more comfortable with risk than passive investors. This section also includes individuals who flip houses often, and those who buy properties for rental income.

Active investors are very knowledgeable about investing and work very hard at it. If this is you, this book will not be enough for you and you'll need a more mathematical and in-depth book on investing.

Passive Investors

This is me and probably most readers. Passive investors are typically more hands-off when it comes to investing. They want to make money, but also keep their money as safe as possible and their minds as sane as possible. The goal for these individuals is to put money into something and watch it grow, with minimal interference and few transactions. They don't want to look at investing information every day. These are the people that only buy or sell investments every few months or even once a year, on a pre-determined schedule.

Definitions of Investment Vehicles
(Actually super important and is the basis of all this investing stuff so please read it)

Stocks

Stocks are pieces of a company that you can own. When you pay money to purchase a stock, you own a portion of the company's assets, liabilities, and income. You're also generally entitled to vote on any issues brought up at something called a shareholder's meeting. Generally, your voice on these matters is trivial, but it's nice to know you have some say, right? But you don't own stock to direct the company, you own stock because you believe the value of the company will rise, or because you like the amount of money it pays out as dividends (more on this in a second).

Stock comes in two types: Common and Preferred. Common stock is the most common (see what I did there?) of the two, because it has fewer strings attached for the company to provide it to the public. Any dividends attached to it are not set and companies can cancel them at any time, which frequently happens in bad economic times. Preferred stocks are less widespread and come with interesting attributes. Their voting rights are not guaranteed, some don't have any at all. However, their dividends are usually set and are paid right on schedule every year. This, along with being ahead of common shareholders in the bankruptcy line, is the advantage of preferred shares. You'll pay a premium for that safety, though, as preferred shares are usually more expensive than common ones and traded much less often. A preferred share is a nice hybrid of stocks and bonds, which we'll discuss next.

Historically, common shares have yielded the highest rate of return over any other investments. But they are risky. At any time, the company you invested your hard-earned money into can go bankrupt and you'll get nothing. Two wonderful examples of both extremes are the companies Apple and Enron between February 1, 2000 and January 1, 2017.

On February 1, 2000, Enron has a stock price of $71.63[33] per share, Apple was at $3.58 per share[34].

As of January 1, 2017, however, Enron no longer exists. It went bankrupt due to some scandals long ago, all its employees were let go, and their pension plans are now gone. While Apple happily trades at $116.15. That's why you need to diversify!

What Are Dividends?

Dividends are what happens when a company has cash left over at the end of the quarter or year and no productive way to spend it, either because they have no good projects available or because they prefer to make their owners happy. Either way, this creates a regular cash giveaway to shareholders. Having stock that pays dividends is a surefire way to get an income from your investments, but not all stocks pay dividends. Whether they do or not depends on the type of company it is.

Type of Companies
Blue Chip

Blue chip describes stock of companies that are huge, stable, and you've most likely heard of them. The Microsofts, IBMs, and RBCs of the world. These companies are so big that any meaningful percentage growth is impossible. $10 million of growth may be a huge deal to a company only worth $100 million, but it's nothing to a company worth $100 billion. Because of this, they typically give a lot of cash to their investors since they simply have no better use for it. Growth in these companies is slow, but very stable. The expectation is that these companies will rarely go out of business and will keep slowly growing for decades to come, so investing in them is quite safe (as far as stocks go).

The way people make money from these is through dividends or buying them at a temporarily low price like during a recession where the entire stock market is on sale.

Growth Stocks

Growth companies put all their money into growing larger and larger. These companies don't usually pay dividends and are aggressively investing in the price of their stock, because they have projects that they believe will create large growth in the company, and they have the room to grow. However, due to this focus on growth the company's stock price can fluctuate widely. The stock prices of these companies are decided solely on the perception of the company and whether it has met the growth goals it set out for itself in the past. If it did great, but less than the stated goal, the stock price might go down regardless of the great performance. In a recession, growth stocks take a much larger hit than blue chip stocks as investors become very pessimistic during those tough times.

The main way to benefit from investing in these types of stocks is to purchase them as soon as possible and sell them as late as possible, to capture the biggest increase in stock price over time as they grow.

Cyclical Stocks

These are companies whose stock goes up and down in predictable patterns depending on their line of business. Examples are companies that make large equipment, or high end product companies. Both of these would be worth more in a growing market and less in a recession. There are also companies that have business cycles unrelated to the market itself, but respond to certain events. Natural disasters can have significant effects on insurance and home building stocks.

To make money from these, you would need to buy them at the bottom of their business cycles and sell at the top. This can be very difficult, and trying to guess the timing of the market in this way is very risky behaviour.

Defensive Stocks

Defensive companies perform well or even great in a bad stock market. They're nice to have when a recession strikes. Wal-Mart is the best example of a company that has this trait, since the majority of the businesses that benefit from tough economic times, like auto repair shops, are not available on the stock market.

To make money from defensive stocks, you would need to buy them before the recession and sell at their highest towards the worst part of the recession. But again, trying to time the stock market is super risky.

Stock can also be called equity or shares.

Type of investor best served: young or risky investors.

Bonds

Bonds are debt that a company owes someone, plain and simple. Companies issue bonds whenever they need extra money to do something they don't have the money to do at that moment, and will pay some sort of interest to the person or company that is willing to loan them that money. This interest is pre-set and paid at specific intervals throughout the year (usually June and December).

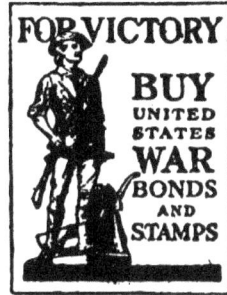

Bonds are safer than stocks in the sense that they're debt, which is paid before stockholders (both common and preferred) in the event of a bankruptcy. But bonds also have low potential for gains; you'll only receive what you lent to the company, plus interest. Bankruptcy has come up a few times in this book. This is because it's the worst case scenario for investors, and it happens more often than you'd think. See the Enron example earlier. Bonds also have their own terminology which can be confusing. Let's go through an example:

Say you have an extra $1,000 hanging out in your bank account and you want to lend it to a company. Along comes Awesome Inc., and they need $1,000,000 to build some cool space lasers. So they take your $1,000 and $999,000 from other people and promise all of you 5% a year paid twice per year in June and December and full repayment in 5 years. The $1,000 you lent Awesome Inc. is called your Principal and is also the Face Value of the bond; you will get this amount back so long as Awesome Inc. doesn't implode. The 5% interest is called a Coupon, and works out to $50 a year. But you get two payments; does that mean you get $50 twice a year? Nope. You'll get $25 each time. At the end of 5 years, the bond's Maturity Date, you'll get your $1,000 back.

The bonds that you'll be buying or selling will rarely come from the company directly. Instead, you'll be trading them on a market or exchange of some sort. There, the situation is not so simple. Bonds can sell at a premium (above) or discount (below) that $1,000 Face Value. The price of bonds on the market can be influenced by many things, but the most important is the interest rate set by the Central Bank of the country. When the Central Bank raises its interest rate, the price of bonds drops because now money can be borrowed from the government at a higher rate, thereby lowering the bond's riskiness. When Central Bank rates are lowered, the reverse happens. Another aspect of bonds that sell on markets is the Yield to Maturity. This is the total amount of interest you'll get if you hold onto the bond until the principal is returned to you, plus (minus) any premium (discount) that was in place when you bought it. The calculation is complicated and we won't get into it here, the higher the better though.

Bonds also come in a number of safety rankings, called bond ratings. Agencies around the world assess the likelihood that the bonds will not be paid back, called a default. These go from AAA to C, with AAA being the highest quality and C being something called a Junk Bond. Junk Bonds can be riskier than stocks, with high interest rates, but also a high possibility of default.

Other names: Bills (less than 1 year maturity), Notes (1-5 year maturity), Bonds (5+ year maturity).

Type of investor best served: older or less risk tolerant investors.

Guaranteed Investment Certificates (GICs)

GICs are pretty similar to bonds, but much less risky. GIC's have principals and interest rates that are paid at whatever interval you choose (monthly, quarterly, or annually).

The interesting part of GICs is that both your principal and the interest it promised you are guaranteed by the government, hence the name. No muss no fuss with this one, except you can't withdraw them for the entire duration of the investment, which is a bit annoying.

These are very simple investments that have quite a low rate of return. There is a somewhat advanced way to create a slightly better return though.

GIC Laddering

The downside to GICs is the problem of locking up your money for a specified amount of time, be it a year or three, without knowing what the interest rates will be in the future. You could come out ahead or behind, depending on where interest rates move during the term of your GIC.

In order to alleviate some of the uncertainty, you have the option of doing something called a GIC Ladder. It spreads your money out across several different lengths of investment, and since you'll be receiving money throughout, you'll be able to take advantage of higher rates. If the rates change, you haven't lost as much money.

To do this, you'll need to spread out the money you have available into GICs with different terms. Usually the ones with longer terms have better rates, which is what entices people to lock in their money for a long time. If you have $5,000 to invest, instead of putting it all in five year GICs and risking losing out on a huge interest rate increase for five years, you can split the money into five $1,000 GICs with the following terms: one year, two year, three year, four year, and five year.

Type of investor best served: older or less risk tolerant investors.

Real Estate

This one is fairly obvious. Real estate is residential buildings (homes, apartments, townhouses, etc.), office buildings, retail buildings (the building with the Timmie's in it, for example), and buildings that are both residential and commercial (nursing homes are a good example). That's a lot of types of real estate. But let's be real, unless you're a multimillionaire already (why would you be reading this?), you're only going to have one type of property to deal with, the residential building, more specifically your house or apartment if you buy it and maybe an investment property or two.

Real estate is a very common investment both for personal reasons (you need somewhere to live) and for money reasons (everybody loves to say that real estate always goes up). So let's talk about it a bit from the money perspective, since we've already talked about how to choose whether to rent or buy in the personal finance section earlier.

The majority of well-meaning people will tell you that real estate is the safest investment. The sales pitch is easy and common: my friend/aunt/son/mom bought their house 20 years ago and now it's worth 400 times that value! That's lovely, and it does happen often.

So, there's a safe and perfect investment, why should we care about the others?

Because there are negatives in real estate investing that are rarely discussed, and they're not insignificant. But before I trash the personal residence as an investment vehicle, let's talk positives. Housing is a very stable investment; homes rarely lose half their value in one day, whereas on the stock market this happens thousands of times every single day. When you sell your home, the transaction is probably tax free. More on this in the tax section. That's right, hundreds of thousands of dollars, tax free. The value of your house can also be taken 'out' of it by borrowing from its value if you need a quick loan for whatever reason (not recommended, but possible).

And now the negatives. The housing market in any given area is sensitive. It can fluctuate based on the interest rate set by the

Central Bank in the country it's in, crime statistics, incomes of the individuals who live in the neighbourhood, jobs available in the area, proximity to infrastructure and shopping, etc. These are things you have no control over. Let's look at Chicago's real estate market over the little while from 1987 to mid-2010. I tried to find a Canadian example but data was hard to find, please forgive me. Look at that ridiculous drop at the end there. I bet you most people who bought a few months earlier thought the prices would just keep rising. The possibility of this type of scenario in any housing market is real and very scary.

Chicago Home Price Index 1995-2010

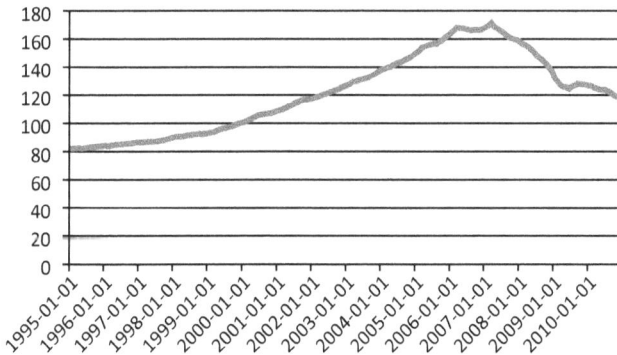

35

Houses are generally quite expensive too, so much so that most people take huge loans worth several times their annual income over 30 years to pay for them (the mortgages we talked about in the personal finance section). When considering the costs of a home, you should also account for the costs of insurance, paying a real estate agent, a lawyer, appraisals, land transfer tax, and property taxes.

What if you bought your house with cash, you say? Well in that case that's awesome! But would it have been the best use of the money? The answer varies. If we use the Detroit chart again, let's say you bought a detached house in 1988 for $100,000 and sold it in January 2007 for $280,000.That's a big jump, 180%.

Annually, that's 10% a year which is amazing, but the U.S. stock market returned 538% over that same time period, almost 30% per year. And that's during a good housing market. If you bought at the top and sold at the bottom, yikes.

What about rental properties? All of the above applies here too, with some additional information. Rental properties are not tax free upon sale, and you have to pay taxes on any income you make through them, so that sucks. But they can be a really good business if you have a place in an area with high rents, but low housing prices. If you have some home maintenance skills, you'll do even better since you won't have to hire contractors every time something breaks. The tenants will pay your mortgage and you'll be out ahead. Many people do very well in areas with universities and colleges where tenants come and go and rents can be increased every year with no issues.

As with everything, there are positives and negatives. Landlords are responsible for repairs and maintenance of a property. If the refrigerator stops working, you have to buy a new one. This can wipe out an entire year's profit. You must also occasionally deal with tenants who are not the nicest people, some might stop paying rent and some might destroy your property. The laws in most areas are also strongly in favour of the tenant, so a landlord's legal powers may be limited.

The largest potential for downside is being on the hook for the mortgage when money is not coming in. This can happen when you have multiple mortgages to pay for different properties and lose tenants, and then you yourself will be responsible for those payments. It can also happen on a larger scale when the housing market in a particular area is in decline, and the home becomes worth less than what remains on your mortgage; it goes 'underwater'. This can happen to a personal residence as well, but it is much worse with multiple properties. You'll be responsible for paying back a mortgage on multiple properties that are guaranteed to lose you money in the short term.

I've included some more information on real estate investing in the investment assessment section later on.

Type of investor best served: investors who can handle the risk and have the cash reserves to pay for the mortgage if the tenants leave.

Whew that was a lot of negativity. Let's move on to simpler things, shall we?

Packaged Instruments

Now we're getting into the more complex packaged instruments, where some company grouped a bunch of stocks or bonds (assets) together and sold a piece of that package to you. That's basically what a mutual fund is. But before we get into that, let's drop some vocabulary that we'll need to understand in order to buy and sell packaged instruments like mutual funds, ETFs, REITs, and any new, fancy instrument that will probably be created before this book goes to print.

Diversification

We've mentioned it before, but this is how you 'spread out' investments in terms of riskiness to avoid any one company's bankruptcy having a large impact on your money. Packaged instruments were made for this purpose as they are literally just that: a package of investments that shields you from having only one company's stock.

Liquidity

We've talked about liquidity before too, but in case you forgot, here is it again. Liquidity is the ability to move your investments around, get rid of them when you need the cash, and buy them back when you don't need your cash anymore. All instantly, without waiting for agents, funds in escrow, lawyers, brokers, or other people to give you the go ahead to do so. Packaged instruments are a little lower in liquidity than plain stocks or bonds because the number of people who buy and sell a specific packaged instrument are lower than the mob that buys and sells a particular company's stock. Unless you're looking at very specific and exotic packaged instruments, this is not generally a big issue.

Transaction Fees

Brokerages charge you a fee every time you move your investments around. When you buy and sell something you'll be charged a certain amount of money. How much depends on the company you use as your brokerage. We'll discuss how to choose one later.

Management Expense Ratios (MERs)
Exactly what they sound like. The people who manage your packaged instruments rack up expenses and you must pay for them. This includes their salaries, the physical office, the marketing they do, and everything in between. The lower these are, the better, because they take away from your earnings every year, and that adds up.

A high MER like 1.5% versus a low one like 0.06% can be the difference between $15,144.21 or $600.18[36] in fees over ten years.

DRIP (Dividend Reinvestment Plan)
This is the concept of being allowed to take any dividends you receive from a certain investment and immediately reinvest them back into more shares of the same thing. The advantage with this strategy is that they're done free of transaction fees, saving you money in the long run if you want to keep increasing the amount of investments you already have.

Mutual Funds

The good thing about mutual funds is that you just buy one and do nothing, it's quick and it's easy. Some professional manager will buy and sell stocks and bonds as they like and fill your mutual fund with assets that will generate money for you. It's also generally good for diversification purposes, since the assets are usually spread out across multiple companies. This reduces the risk of your mutual fund losing all its value if one company disappears. Since they are bought and sold outside of regular work hours only, the shares of the fund are of medium liquidity.

Now for the bad. Mutual funds are fairly expensive due to the high pay of the professional manager, the fancy brochures, and the commission paid to sales people. This translates into a higher MER than other packaged instruments like ETFs. There's also the widespread notion that mutual funds don't do any better than the stock market they operate in[37], which means buying them over something like an ETF might be a moot point.

A mutual fund can have any type of direction in its asset buying. Some focus on certain parts of the world (like a country or region), specific industries, or trying to replicate entire stock markets. It's like Rule 34 of the internet, but with Mutual Funds. If you can think of it, there's a mutual fund for it[38].

Type of investor best served: anyone and everyone, mutual funds are all over the map in terms of risk profile and the assets they hold. The easiest way to gauge whether they're right for you is to assess your riskiness like we did before, with a split of stocks and bonds, and look at the holdings to see how closely they come to your ideal allocation.

Real Estate Investment Trusts (REITs)

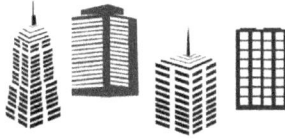

REITs are the mutual funds of the real estate world, a package of properties or mortgages. 'But', you say, 'don't you hate real estate?' Not at all. It's an investment with pros and cons like any other. REITs are a way to lessen the cons of owning your own real estate, and I'm all for reducing the negatives of any investment. There are REIT's for apartment buildings, agricultural land, and even senior care facilities. Whatever money they make from these properties, be it rent or appreciation in value, gets pushed out to you when you own a REIT.

The great thing about these is diversification. No one building will destroy the value of your investment, and you'll be able to weather many market downturns since real estate is not strongly correlated with stocks or bonds. REITs also pay out a good income, since many are legally required to release at least 90% of their income to their shareholders. REITs are traded on markets similar to stocks, and are therefore very liquid and easy to buy and sell if the need arises. Costs associated with REITs would be the same as the ones associated with mutual funds, with MERs moving up or down depending on the level of management's involvement in the trust.

Type of investor best served: individuals who want to invest in real estate but not through a personally owned property.

Exchange-Traded Funds (ETF)

ETFs are the new cool kid on the block. They're like mutual funds, literally the exact same thing. So what makes them different?

Originally, they were invented to be a way around mutual fund managers taking huge salaries for barely beating the stock market's returns. So instead, ETFs mirror the stock market itself. ETFs have investments in assets that represent whatever companies that the market they try to replicate has in it. For example, an ETF that tracks the Toronto Stock Exchange (TSX) will own all the major companies that are listed on it in the right amounts to best approximate the market. The theory is that if the TSX does well, so will the ETF based on it.

This investment strategy does not involve constant buying and selling or decision making on the fund manager's side so ETFs are generally much cheaper to operate and therefore have lower MERs than mutual funds.

The benefits of ETFs are similar to mutual funds: easy to buy and sell and very diversified in their holdings. With low management involvement and a clear index tracking strategy, the added bonus with ETFs is much lower costs.

Nowadays, ETFs are becoming the mutual funds of the future. The new ETFs have high MERs and specialized holdings that appeal to various types of investors. These are no better than mutual funds, and should be carefully appraised for their value against their mutual fund cousins. If you're interested in a passive strategy, select one of the ETFs that stick closer to their original intention.

Type of investor best served: same as Mutual Funds.

And we're finally done with definitions. Now you know what you can invest in, but how should you divide your money among all these choices? Let's go back to that investor profile we were talking about earlier.

Back to Risk Profiles

Let's go back to the risk profile you determined for yourself a while back. You're either open to high risk, medium risk, or only happy with low risk. How do the investment types compare?

High Risk	Individual Stocks Multiple Real Estate Holdings
Risky	ETFs REITs Mutual Funds
Medium Risk	One Real Estate Holding
Low Risk	Bonds GICs

Most people prefer a mix of different risk-rated investments, so they can create a portfolio that fits their knowledge and risk level most accurately. The easiest way to look at how all these types of investments fit together in one person's portfolio is to show many examples of different situations.

Example Portfolios

Meet Jessica. She's 25, has a very stable but busy job at a law firm and makes $70,000. She has no immediate plans for owning a house and currently enjoys the freedom of renting. She feels that she has a lot of appetite and patience for risky investments. She has savings of $10,000. What should she do?

Well, she doesn't need a large emergency fund due to her job situation, so she'll keep a month of expenses on hand in a High Interest Savings Account which pays 1.5% interest. That's $1,700 gone (let's say that's her monthly basic expenses).

Next, she'll put the rest in her TFSA since she has $52,000 to use up (TFSA contribution limit if you were 18 in 2009). She has no money left over to contribute to an RRSP. She should prioritize the TFSA since her income will grow in the future. How will her investments be divided within the TFSA?

- 10% bonds will provide stability to her portfolio
- 90% ETFs that track the world stock market will round out the rest of her portfolio. Jessica chose the world stock market to get good exposure with the least amount of work

She chose ETFs because she has no time or financial knowledge to choose individual stocks, and feels that the lower MERs of the ETFs she found are a better choice than mutual funds. She feels she has the time to watch her portfolio grow for many years without withdrawing anything, so she is comfortable with the high focus on stocks.

Say hello to Justin. He's also 25 and loves apartment life. His job as a welder would make him a lot of money at $100,000 a year if he worked full time, but work is not easy to get and he sometimes spends months unemployed. As a result, he's sensitive to his money losing value since he might need it at any moment. He has $70,000 saved up and doesn't know what to do with it.

Since he's not consistently employed, he should have a healthy emergency fund that could take him through a long period of unemployment. If he is commonly unemployed for stretches of 2-4 months at a time, 6 months of expenses would be able to carry him through a particularly bad year. If his expenses are the same as Jessica's, that would be $10,200 that would go into a high interest savings account.

After that, he'll split his remaining $59,800 in the following way: $52,000 to maximize his TFSA and the remaining $7,800 into his RRSP provided he has the room (having had to previously earn $43,300 in his life). His investments will be divided in the following way:

- 40% bonds will provide stability
- 10% REITs that will provide him with income and a different risk type than stocks
- 10% dividend producing ETFs which will be slightly less risky than normal market following ETFs and provide him with regular income
- 40% ETFs that track the world stock market will round out the rest of his portfolio

As much as possible, he should keep the REITs and Bonds in his RRSP and the rest in his TFSA. We'll discuss why in a few pages.

This is Justin's older sister Amanda, aren't they adorable? She's 30 years old and in the market for a home purchase in the next year or two. She works a high-ranking job at a bank and earns $80,000 per year. Because of her work, she's exposed to the ups and downs of the stock market quite often, and would prefer to take a balanced approach to have some risk, but not too much. She has $100,000 saved up.

While her work is consistent, it's not a guarantee. Her emergency fund would be acceptable at 2 months' worth of income at $3,400. But Amanda is saving for a big purchase! If she's looking to buy a $350,000 condominium apartment, she'd need a down payment of $70,000 to keep somewhere safe for her purchase. This only leaves her with $26,600 to invest.

In Amanda's case, it might be a good idea to put her savings in her RRSP instead of her TFSA due to her high income and low potential for it to go much higher (since her job is already high-ranking). To satisfy her medium risk profile, her investments could be arranged as follows:

- 40% Bonds will provide stability
- 60% ETFs that track the world stock market to provide growth potential

Amanda shouldn't invest in REITs since her home will be the real estate portion of her portfolio.

Relationships Between Investment Types

Despite being open to risk, our example portfolios held bonds. Why is that? These investment types provide stability for a portfolio in the event of a recession or a bad stock market period. Bond investments generally go up during downturns while stocks go down. As a result, many people keep them in their portfolios to provide a steadying effect during those times.

Real estate serves the same purpose, despite being a riskier asset than bonds, especially when invested in through a REIT or multiple rental properties. It is not strongly correlated with the stock market, meaning it won't go down with the stock market. This gives your portfolio a bit of protection. But real estate might not go up during a recession either, since real estate is influenced by the local market more than anything.

How to Assess Investments

How should you go about picking different investments? Below are some examples of metrics you can use to compare different investments to each other to decide which ones are the best for your portfolio.

Earnings per Share (EPS): This metric measures what amount each share would receive if the company paid out all of its profit to its shareholders. It would be a ridiculous situation, but the idea allows you to compare the profitability of different companies in the same industry.

Ex: if company A made $100 million this year and had 10 million shares, its EPS is $10 ($100/10). Company B's EPS would be $5 if it made the same $100 million this year but had 20 million shares on the market.

Price to Earnings (P/E) ratio: Measures how the price of the investments relates to its earnings. This calculation can suggest if the stock is over or under priced compared to its peers in the industry.

Ex: Company A has a Stock Price of $100 and EPS of $10, Company B has a Stock Price of $100 and an EPS of $20, Company A would have a PE ratio of 10 ($100/10) and Company B would have a PE ratio of 5 ($100/20). In comparable companies, the lower the PE ratio the better (in general).

Dividend Payout Ratio: How much the investment pays in dividends to its owners compared to its earnings. This calculation allows you to check how 'healthy' the dividends are, and if the company is making enough money to support its dividend. Blue Chip stocks will have a higher dividend payout ratio while growing companies will have a lower ratio, due to their uses of their cash as described before.

Ex: If a company has a dividend of $1 and an EPS of 5, the payout ratio would be 20% (1/5).

Dividend Yield: How much the investment pays in dividends to its owners in relation to its stock price. The calculation allows you to compare the amount of cash that flows to you from each investment you have, showing you the most 'profitable' ones based on the cash flow alone. Whether a high dividend yield is good or bad depends on your intentions. If you like having a high income, then it's perfect. If you like companies to invest in themselves, then a high dividend yield is not so great.

Ex: Company A has a stock price of $50 and Company B has a stock price of $100, both pay $1 per share. Company A has a dividend yield of 2% (1/50) and Company B has a dividend yield of 1% (1/100).

Price to Rent Ratio: Measures your potential rent income against the price of the property. In order to calculate this metric you need to divide the median home price in the area by the median annual rent amount. As a general rule of thumb, you should buy when this ratio is below 15. Anything above 20 would generally not be considered a good rental investment opportunity.

Ex: A property that rents out at $2,000 per month and costs $500,000 would have a Price to Rent ratio of 20.8, signifying a less than appetizing investment. If the rent in the area was $3,000 per month instead, it would be a much more interesting investment at a ratio of 13.8.

Net Rental Yield: This metric measures the profitability of your property. To calculate it, you should take your potential rental income less all operating expenses (repairs costs, taxes, insurance, agency fees, etc.), and then divide that number by the total cost of the property. The result can be multiplied by 100 in order to get a percentage.

These assessment ratios and figures are not the be-all and end-all of assessing investments. There are so many more out there. These are meant to familiarize you with some of the language that surrounds investing and give you a small taste of it.

Debt versus Investment

If you have debt like student loans or a mortgage, should you still invest?

We've talked about debt as a whole before, but this is a tough question for a lot of people. The way I like to think of debt is that it's like investing, but backwards. Instead of being paid interest for lending your money to a company or earning income for owning a company, you're the one paying someone interest to give you money.

Framed this way, it all depends on how much you think you'll earn if you invested the money instead of using it to pay down debt. Let's say you have $500 to spend. If you have a credit card balance of $1,000 that you pay 20% interest, or you could invest in a dividend paying stock that provides 3.5% of its stock value in dividends. If you pay down the debt, you'll earn 20% on your money in the form of not having to pay that interest anymore, or $100 of extra money now that you're free from the obligation of that interest. Is it money coming in? No, but now it's not money going out. If you had invested in that stock you'd have received $17.50, but would have still had to pay the $100 in interest on the credit card. In this case if you had invested instead of paying down the debt, you'd end up losing money so investing would have been a bad choice.

The rational decision should come down to the rate of interest you're paying on your debt versus the rate of return in either dividends, interest, or price growth you think you'll achieve with the investment. The issue with this approach is that while the debt 'return' is guaranteed, the investment returns are not. Dividends can be reduced at the company's will, the market might crash, anything can happen. Loans like student loans and mortgages that were issued at a great rate are generally debt that is safe-ish to carry. Depending on your investment possibilities and financial situation, your options should be reassessed often.

Regardless of rationality, many people find a huge amount of comfort in being debt free. If that's you, there's no amount of return that can make up for that feeling. That's perfectly fine and you should pay down as much debt as possible in this case. Peace of mind is more important than a 2% difference in investment returns.

Dividend versus Index Investing

To reap the biggest future benefit, should your investments provide dividends or price growth? We're going to compare two common investing strategies: dividend investing (buying stocks that pay good dividends), and index investing (buying all the companies that many up a certain country's stock market). Which one should you go with?

It's a common question and it doesn't have a black and white answer. I'll do my best to assess both sides of the argument.

Before I go into pros and cons, let's talk similarities. Both strategies generally go for 'buy and hold' approaches, where transactions are low and the companies that are being invested in are not on the super risky side of things. The difference between your final portfolio values will not be staggering.

Dividend investing is great because it provides you with a (hopefully) steady stream of income and a small increase in the value of your investment over time as the companies slowly grow. In a recession, you'd still be receiving dividends. Compared to the others whose portfolio values will decrease dramatically, your portfolio will keep some of its value. It's possible that the dividends might get reduced due to the difficult times though. The downside to dividend investing is the amount of work that goes into researching companies and the relative financial sophistication required. You need to know and understand yields and technical analysis, as well as choose the right companies, or funds of companies, for your portfolio and risk level. This results in slightly more active investing with increased transaction costs if an investment reduced its dividend below an acceptable level or you found a new one you like. There are ETFs that will do this for you, but their MERs are in the high range.

Pros: Steady income stream, less movement in a recession.

Cons: More research and effort needed, potentially higher transaction costs.

Index investing is great because it requires no research into individual stocks, just the initial research into which fund you'd like to work with. After that, you pour money in and wait.

Generally, a small dividend will be received in this case as well, due to the nature of the companies that make their way into indexes (big, strong, and long-lasting). In this way, index investing contains a bit of dividend investing without meaning to. Another benefit is while both methods include large and stable companies, index investing also includes smaller companies. This is advantageous because a lot of the growth in a stock market comes from these smaller companies. Apple and Google weren't always behemoths.

The largest downside is the risk that your investment's value will tank if the market does, which it will. This situation requires nerves of steel and a resolve not to sell your shares, and even the nerve to put more money in. Another downside of index investing is that the cash you'll earn will be imaginary unless you go and sell some stocks. This is an issue for people that need or want constant income (retired individuals are a good example, or the temporarily unemployed). Index investing is also very boring, for those who want investing to be an exciting pastime.

Pros: Not much research, small steady income, lower transaction costs.

Cons: Risk of temporarily losing value in the event of a recession, low income without selling off shares.

Choosing a Brokerage

What is a brokerage? It's a company that allows you to invest your money. Most investments need to be bought and sold through a brokerage, since the investing infrastructure hasn't evolved to the point where you can walk up to Apple headquarters with $10,000 and say 'Give me some shares!' You have four options when it comes to brokerages.

Financial Advisor

This is the stereotypical bank employee or independent advisor that helped your parents get their mortgage, and who they go to meet with once in a while to discuss 'investments'.

These individuals offer personalized investing plans catered to your goals and one-on-one discussions about your finances. They can be great and very knowledgeable. However, the downside to this level of attention and coziness is that these individuals are usually trained in a very particular way to get you to give quite a bit of money away to them through commissions. They don't mean to steer you towards these investments, it's just how they're trained and all they know. They have a limited set of investments to offer you and those happen to make the bank lots of money. So, the upsides are personalized attention and advice, with the downsides being high commissions on transactions or investments with high MERs. To get personalized attention and counteract the MER cost, you can consult a fee-based financial advisor. These are individuals that give advice and personalized investment plans, but get no commissions or fees from the investments; you pay them by the hour.

Personal Financial Advisors are good to have at the beginning of the investing journey when you're not that knowledgeable, scared of investing, and need someone to hold your hand. I'm hoping this book helps steer you away from these.

Bank Hosted

These are accounts within your bank where you hold money that you want to invest and where those investments live as well. The idea is that your bank creates an easy transaction to transfer money from your chequing account to your investing account.

Banks rarely offer consultations or any guidance on what to do with this money since they offer financial advising services. Banks make money on these accounts in one of two ways: transaction fees and bank-specific investments. Transaction fees are pretty standard stuff, you pay $X for every buy or sell transaction you make in this account. The bank-specific investments are more interesting. The bank generally gives you incentives to buy them by making the transaction fees for these investments lower than others, or even $0. Where the bank makes money is the MERs, similar to the situation above. Sometimes, the MERs are comparable to other options outside the bank though, so they might just be a good deal.

As long as you're careful with the investments you choose to make in these types of accounts and keep transactions to a minimum, these are a great place to put your investments. The link with your bank account will make transferring money easier and create a better customer profile for you at the bank.

Independent Brokerage

Normally these are online only institutions where you hold money and investments. This type of account is more or less the same as the one above; you have no guidance in investing and the account is there for you to buy and sell investments without supervision.

Where the independent brokerages have the advantage is the cost to the investor. The brokerages usually make their money in paid-for investing guidance (similar to a fee investor), or in putting fees on specialized trading strategies and investments.

These will hopefully not apply to you. As a result, the per transaction cost of these brokerages is usually lower than the bank-sponsored ones above. You are also not guided towards any specific investment, allowing you to buy whatever investments work best for you.

As long as you know which investments you want and have a strong strategy behind you, these accounts are great and the cheapest way to invest. My job with this book is to make sure you have the knowledge and confidence to use them. But you don't have to, the other options are valid as well.

Robo Advisor

Robo advisors are a new breed of investment situation that very recently came into existence. They are a combination of financial advisors and independent brokerages.

Robo advisors use an algorithm that buys and sells investments for you based on a questionnaire, and maybe a phone interview, you do when you open the account. The questionnaire will go over your risk profile, time horizons, preferences for types of investments, etc. It'll be painless and easy. After you open the account you generally put money in through your bank like paying a bill. The robo advisors charge you a certain percentage of the total value of your account, as well as any fees on the investments they buy for you. The good thing here is that usually they try to keep it to low MER investments and generally don't have that many transactions outside of investing every time you put money in.

I believe this is the second best option outside of the independent brokerages described above. The fees to manage funds are much smaller than a human advisor would charge. Results will vary depending on your answers to the questionnaire.

Choosing a brokerage is a personal choice, and the only difference between the do-it-yourself and advisor approaches is the control you have over what you invest in. It's your job to decide how much control you want and are comfortable with.

Taxation on Investment Income

Taxes! The most fun you'll ever have with a calculator or Excel spreadsheet.

Canadian Dividends

Dividends from investments are included in the individual's regular income when they are received, but not at the amount they were received at. Dividends in Canada are weird, in a good way.

Eligible Dividends

When you receive these kinds of dividends, the total amount you'll report on your tax return will be 138% of the amount you received. Don't freak out, you'll get a credit to offset it. The credit is around 15% (federal) of the total amount you got above after the gross up, depending on the province you live in.

Non Eligible Dividends

Dividends that, in their previous life as corporate profits, were taxed at a rate called the Small Business Deduction. It's not really important to know why or how that is calculated, just to know why these get taxed more than the others. The gross up is 117% and the tax credit is 10.52% (federal).

The Famous $50,000 Tax Free From Dividends

Is it possible to get $50,000 of dividends without paying any taxes? Kind of, depending on where you live and how much other income you have.

If $50,000 of eligible dividends is your only income and you live in Alberta, British Columbia, New Brunswick, Northwest Territories, Nunavut, Ontario, Saskatchewan, or the Yukon, you're good to go. Otherwise you'll be paying some taxes in the other provinces and on any income over $50,000 regardless of where it comes from.

Foreign Income

Foreign income is any income (dividends or interest) you receive from investments whose home base is not Canada. When it comes to foreign income, there is something called a withholding tax that you might want to be aware of. Withholding tax is a tax applied to income paid to foreign investors at the source of the investment before being sent to that investor overseas. The amount of tax taken off the top varies, but it's taken from the earnings only. You will not have to pay a fee outside of that.

Some countries like the U.S. have treaties with Canada which will waive this withholding tax if you hold investments in a very particular way. In our case it's holding U.S. stocks (including ETFs) in an RRSP account. You may also be able to reduce or get rid of this tax by claiming a special tax credit, which we'll discuss in the tax section ahead.

Interest

Interest from bonds or other debt is calculated into regular income either when it is announced that you'll receive it or when you actually receive it. There is a choice in this matter that you must make for each investment and keep for the life of that investment.

There could be a situation where the bond may say it pays interest on June 15 and December 15, but the money might not make it to you until January 4. In the first options, you would still pay tax on the income. Or you could choose to pay the tax in the January year. Either way it is added to your employment income and others to be taxed at your personal marginal tax rate, which we'll acquaint you with a few sections from now.

You are also allowed to deduct some expenses from this income if applicable:
- Investment advising fees
- Costs incurred to obtain a loan (legal fees and mortgage appraisal fees), split over five years equally

- Fees for managing your investments or holding your securities
- Accounting fees for keeping records of your income

Rental Income

Income from renting out land or property you own is included in your regular income as it's earned, not when it's paid.

If you have a tenant that's late on his or her December rent and pays it on January 3rd instead of December 1st, you still have to include that payment in the prior year's income because you were owed it. This can create a very nasty situation where you may be paying taxes on income you're not getting if you have a bad tenant.

The expenses you're allowed to deduct from this income are:

- Interest on your mortgage
- Costs required to obtain a loan (legal fees and mortgage appraisal fees), split over five years equally
- Insurance expenses
- Property taxes
- Maintenance costs (lawn care, garbage removal, etc.)
- Landscaping
- Depreciation
- Property management fees

If there's a loss for the year where expenses outweigh the income, you might be able to apply it to reduce other incomes in the year (employment, business income, capital gains).

For those looking at owning a rental property, you need to do some serious math with an eye to taxes to make sure you can deduct everything, and are within the tax rules about investment properties and losses.

Capital Gains
Regular Investments

When the price you paid for an investment initially is lower than the price you sold it for, you create capital gains.

The way taxes on this gain are calculated is to only include half of the total gain in your income, called the taxable capital gain, which is then taxed at your regular tax rate. This is one of the simplest tax situations.

Brokerage and transaction fees are deductible from capital gains for tax purposes.

Lifetime Capital Gains Exemption

The words above mean that you could receive $835,716(2017 amount) of a specific type of capital gains, for free. Crazy!

Before you get too excited, they only apply to very specific investments that you are unlikely to make unless you're an entrepreneur or a farmer. You'd have to have sold shares of something called a Qualified Small Business Corporation or farming or fishing property.

Principal Residence Exemption

This is another gift from the government of Canada. If you've sold a house and have lived in it the time you've owned it, the whole gain is tax free.

The property doesn't have to be in Canada and you don't have to live in it for the whole year, just at some point during. You may only have one 'Principal Residence' per year though, so if you have a second property you need to decide which to claim for that particular year.

The principal residence exemption formula is:

$$\frac{(\text{\# of years investment is principal residence} + 1)}{\text{\# of years investment is owned}} \times \text{capital gain}$$

If you rented out the same home as a rental property, you can now only designate the property as a principal residence for 4 years.

Capital Losses

A capital loss happens when you sell an investment for less than you paid for it. Capital losses can be used to cancel out capital gains or reduce the amount of gains that are subject to tax. Any unused gains can be carried 3 years back in time and forward indefinitely.

The definitions above are a bit sparse and are more of a primer. We'll go over how much you'd pay on each of these income types and other details in the tax section.

Where Should You Hold Your Investments?

Now that we've learned how different investment income behaves at tax time, let's take a look at which investments go where. You have two main, tax-friendly investment accounts which we've talked about in the savings section, but I didn't tell you what to put in them to minimize taxes.

Before we discuss the investments themselves, make sure to maximize all your tax-friendly accounts first. There's rarely a reason to hold anything outside of those accounts unless you have no room left. Another thing not to do is pick investments based on their tax properties, taxes are only a side effect of making money. The important part about investments is to grow your money in a way you're comfortable with. Investing in dividend producing stocks when you'd be more comfortable with bonds just because dividends have a better tax treatment does not make sense.

RRSP & TFSA

Tax sheltered accounts are a great place for interest producing assets like bonds and GICs, due to the relatively harsh treatment of income from those investments, being taxed at your marginal tax rate.

If you hold any REITs, they should be held in tax sheltered accounts due to their awkward situation. REITs give out a lot of different kinds of income. They provide capital gains, which are easy to deal with, but also return of capital. Return of capital is not taxable at all because it's like principal being returned to you, but it lowers your 'bought at' price for the REIT and therefore creates a bigger capital gain later on. If you hold them outside of tax sheltered accounts, you'll need to meticulously keep track of this. They also give out 'other income' which is fully taxable. Foreign REITs will also have withholding taxes. To avoid this mess, they are best kept in RRSPs and TFSAs.

If you hold U.S. stocks or U.S. based ETFs directly, you should hold them in an RRSP because you won't be subject to withholding taxes on these investments due to a treaty Canada has with the US.

Be very careful about holding investments that will take large losses in a TFSA unless you can offset them with gains. By the nature of this account, any losses will also reduce your total contribution room. If you have $52,000 of room available which you've used to put in highly risky stocks that then lost 50% of their value, which you then took out of the TFSA, when you go back to re-contribute you'll only be able to put in $26,000 instead of the original $52,000.

For all non U.S. foreign investments, try to keep as many of them in tax sheltered from taxes accounts since they are taxed like interest. Do some research on any treaties like the one we have with the U.S to see if you can get a better deal.

Taxable Account

If you plan on receiving capital gains from your investments and have no more room in your tax sheltered accounts, those investments should be quite comfortable in a taxable account due to their lenient treatment come tax time.

You'll also be able to use any capital losses you incur to offset gains, but hopefully you won't have too many of those.

Dividends from Canadian companies are also treated quite well, so the taxable account is a relatively pain free place to hold investments that provide dividends if you have nowhere else to put them.

With foreign investments held here, you will pay withholding taxes, but you'll receive a credit for the amount paid that you can claim on your tax return.

Emotions and Investing

Investing can be pretty scary. Especially
when you invested in a good market and
now you're looking at a 40% drop in
value due to a recession. You might
want to sell to protect against any more
losses, right? That's a dumb move, don't
do it.

Unless you really need the money for whatever reason, don't
take it out. Those losses are not real unless you make them real.
Stocks historically generally go back to their pre-recession levels
in a few years. Holding on will make you no worse off than you
were before the recession, and the recession will give you the
opportunity to buy investments on sale.

People generally buy investments in times when the stock
markets are calm or doing well, spurred on by various information
sources urging them to buy, promising good returns[39]. This
creates a happy feeling of optimism as long as the good returns
keep coming.

However, when a market turns sour and heads down, people
experience panic and fear. They act irrationally without
considering the situation above (that the recession is temporary
and they won't need their retirement funds for decades) and try to
'protect' themselves from declining market values. This can be a
very quick way to lose a lot of money and is completely
unnecessary. When making an investment decision, especially one
to sell an investment, think about whether that decision will
benefit you in the long term or if you're acting on impulse.
Majority of investor behaviour is impulsive, so asking yourself
that question would be a way to mitigate that.

On the other hand, many investors will wait to invest in good
markets. They'll feel that the market is too expensive and wait for
a small dip, thinking they'll outsmart everyone else. This is called
Market Timing. Sometimes that dip does come, other times the
market keeps marching on without you. This will leave you with
regret and a feeling of 'what could have been'. According to
Vanguard, two out of three times you will be better off if you had

just put your money in when you had it than if you waiting to invest it at a particular moment[40]. The best time to invest in was 30 years ago, the next best time is today. So get on that.

Very rarely will you be 100% happy with your investments. Remember that and accept it.

A good investing strategy should try to divorce emotion from your investments as much as possible. Create a schedule and an allocation you feel comfortable with and carry on, regardless of what the market does. This strategy is called Dollar Cost Averaging and is good for all market conditions. In the long run, the theory is that the market will continue going up, so keep your head down and come along for the ride. Investing on any day in 2017 will look like a bargain in 2035.

Home Country Bias

Home country bias is exactly what it sounds like: holding or tending to hold the majority of investments in your home country's stock market. Why do people do this? Because they feel more comfortable with their country's companies and laws. They hear about them on the news and their government might even pander to these companies. Not so with companies half a world away. People tend to be more optimistic towards what they know and more pessimistic towards the things they know less about; it's the same with investments.

While this tendency creates a more comfortable investor, it might be counterintuitive. In the event that something happens to your home country's financial markets, not having the diversity of investing in other countries could be your downfall as all those investments will lose value and there will be no offsetting growth. It could also keep you from seeing the growth in other areas of the world that could be booming while Canada just floats along. This is unsurprisingly a very common issue, since in 2012 Canadians held 59% of all their stock holdings in Canadian companies[41]. This is kind of ridiculous considering Canadian stocks only make up less than 4% of the world's stock value.

Unless you have strategic reasons not to, it generally makes sense to craft your stock portfolio in line with the world's stock weights by country: the U.S. would have around 50%, 4% to Canada, 20% to Europe, and the rest to the Pacific area. This would be similar to what the Vanguard Total World Stock ETF (VT)[42] holds. This kind of strategy lowers the up and downs (volatility) that your portfolio might suffer since the regions move up and down with different correlations to each other. Some could be losing badly while others are flourishing, but you'll come ahead every time.

There are a few benefits to home country bias that shouldn't be forgotten, though:

Currency risk: when you hold all your investments in Canadian dollars, you can be blissfully unaware of the exchange rate with any other currency. It's simply irrelevant to you. But if you hold the majority of your investments in US dollars while being paid and living your life in Canadian dollars, you will be very sensitive to the exchange rate between the two whenever you put more money in or make a withdrawal. You should know that being invested in other currencies actually adds a layer of diversification as well, but having to worry about currency exchange swings is definitely not fun.

Lower taxes: Canadian dividends are treated like royalty for tax purposes. On the flip side, foreign investment gains usually get a piece taken out by the issuing country through withholding taxes. If you hold these investments in a TFSA or RRSP you won't be able to get that back (unless it a U.S. listed stock in an RRSP). So, not only will having international investments make filing your taxes a huge pain, it'll also take a bite out of profits.

At the end of the day, you're going to do what you're comfortable with. But do me a favour and don't go 100% Canadian investments.

4 Taxes

Do You Need to Pay Taxes?

Everyone's favorite thing about the government is giving them a portion of your hard earned cash. As they say, death and taxes are the only two certainties in life.

Do you pay someone to do your taxes? You probably don't have to. I'll teach you how to do it!

But first, let's drop some knowledge because taxes are not the simplest thing in the world. To keep this conversation simple, I assume the reader is not married and has no children.

Are you Canadian Enough to Pay Taxes?

Or as the Canadian Revenue Agency (CRA) prefers to ask, are you a resident? That's not a question of where your home is, but a weird government created status unrelated to citizenship.

You are automatically a resident if you were in Canada for longer than 182 days in any January to December annual period of time.

If you don't meet the general rule above, you could still be considered a resident, and be liable for taxes, depending on these factors:

1. The amount of time you spend in Canada on a regular basis
2. The reasons behind your movements in and out of Canada (you might be trying to avoid our high tax rates!)
3. Home ownership in Canada and how accessible it is to you
4. Any social and financial connections you have to Canada

These are much more subjective so you would be at the mercy of the CRA, who will determine your status.

Take two different situations for example. Ricardo lives and works in the United States. He has a wife and a daughter that live in a house he owns in Manitoba. He visits his family every weekend and holds investments in Canadian dollars in a Canadian bank. Ricardo will most likely be considered a Canadian resident due to his very strong, continuing relationship with the country.

Now let's look at Mary's situation. She also lives and works in the United States too. She has no spouse or children but her parents and extended family live in Ontario. She visits her family a few times a year for the main holidays. Her Canadian bank accounts and investments still exist but she does not add to them, preferring to put her wages into a U.S. bank account and U.S. investments she holds through U.S. based accounts. She has a property in Ontario that she owns with her parents which is rented out to a tenant on a multi year lease. Mary will likely not be considered a Canadian resident, since her relationship with Canada is not particularly strong. Her visits are infrequent and her home not easily accessible should she want to move back.

So are you a resident? If so, keep reading.

Did you make any money during the year?

Before you answer this question, we must determine what a 'year' means to the CRA.

For individuals, a year is January 1st to December 31st of any given calendar year.

What about 'money'? If you *received* any income during any calendar year you must report it to the CRA, regardless if you did the work to *earn* it in another tax year. Why received and not earned? Taxes are sometimes calculated based on something called Cash Basis Accounting, meaning transactions only count when the cash actually moves around. This creates a very interesting effect where things that happened in one calendar year won't be included in that year's taxes because they didn't actually get paid out until the next year. Some examples would be:

- A bonus announced on December 15, 2016, but paid out on January 15, 2017, would be included in the 2017 taxation year
- Interest or dividend payments that are announced in December but not paid out till February

This is a much larger issue for corporations, but they have the money to hire tax accountants. The issues for individuals are less complicated, but it's good to be aware of the way the system works, so there are no surprises when you do your tax forms. Some income types don't follow this rule and I'll warn you when it comes up.

Types of Income

So what's considered income? A whole slew of things. There are 5 main categories of income that an individual can earn. I'll summarize them here and then go into the nitty gritty of each section's different rules, so you can pick and choose which sections to read depending on which ones apply to you. Most people will only have one or two of the five types.

The nice thing is that if you have income that doesn't fit into any of the categories below, it's not subject to tax. Hello lottery winnings and inheritances!

Employment Income

Employment income is paid to anyone who sells their time or services to an entity (business or individual) for a salary, hourly wage, or benefits. People who sell services on a per service basis and are not controlled by an entity of any kind, like independent contractors, don't fall into this category.

Capital Gains

Capital gains are the proceeds of selling an asset that was not acquired to generate short term income. This is a slightly awkward definition because it does include items like stocks, which can produce short term gains via dividends, but does not include a house that a house flipper (person who buys and sells homes as a way to make a living) might sell. In general, these are the proceeds of selling an asset that was bought in order to make money in the long term or for personal enjoyment.

Property Income

Property income is earned by assets that you own. This includes income from investments (like interest and dividends), rent from real estate, and royalties from any licensed material you own. This category is where 'passive income' comes from, since whatever is generating money for you has already been done and you're just sipping pina coladas in your hammock raking it all in.

Business Income

Business income is an extremely broad category of income. It includes any and all actions, official business or not, that are undertaken in order to earn a profit. This includes running a business from home, mowing a neighbour's lawn for cash, and even selling stuff on Craigslist.

Other Income and Deductions

This category is not as open ended as the title suggests. It specifically only includes the following: pension incomes (including Old Age Security and Canadian Pension Plan distributions), Employment Insurance benefits, alimony payments, RRSP withdrawals, and your company's deferred profit sharing plan distributions.

The deductions side includes RRSP contributions, alimony payments, child care expenses and, moving expenses.

Employment Income, Taxable Benefits, and Deductions

Employees make up the majority of taxpayers in this country, so this type of income most likely applies to almost anybody that will read this book.

An employee is a person that sells their services to an entity for an agreed upon wage, with the services to be provided determined by the entity. An individual who is self-employed can have multiple entities paying for his or her services, and has discretion over how the work is done. Which one you are makes a huge difference on your taxes, since self-employed individuals earn business income, not employment income.

If you're not sure where you stand, the CRA has six factors that they look at to determine if you're an employee or not[43]:

Control

Who makes the decision of when, where, how, and what you do at work? An employer will usually make most, if not all, of these decisions for an employee. An independent contractor will most likely only be told what needs to be done and maybe given some restrictions on when it can be done, but the rest will be up to them.

Tools and Equipment

What tools and equipment do you need to do your job, and who provides them? An employee will have their tools provided by the employer, like a desk with a computer on it. A self-employed individual is usually required to bring their own tools and equipment, like a toolbox for an electrician or a car for an Uber driver.

Subcontracting and Assistants

Are you able to hire someone to do all, or part, of the job for you? Self-employed individuals will usually be able to hire any assistants and subcontractors for the work they're doing to get the job done quicker, or in order to avoid work they can't do. Employees will generally be restricted in their ability to reduce their workload by hiring other people to do the work.

Financial Risk

What type of ongoing costs are associated with your job? Are you being reimbursed for them, or expected to take the loss as an offset to your income? If you have to drive from client to client as a consultant or need special training for your job, do you pay for those costs or does someone reimburse you? If you're reimbursed, it's likely you're an employee. Self-employed individuals will be able to deduct these costs against their income as the cost of doing business.

Opportunity for profit

Is it possible for you to make a profit or a loss through your work? As an employee, you generally earn a salary or wage no matter what happens to the business (provided you're not fired due to a bad year). As a self-employed person, you're in charge of every aspect of the situation, so a profit or loss is entirely up to you.

If any of these considerations are conflicting, just compare how many are for employment and against. The winning side will be your answer.

Employment Income Defined

What gets included in your employment income? More than you would expect:

1. All compensation from your employment situation: salaries, wages, commissions, and gratuities (yes, tips are taxable)
2. All benefits you receive due to employment (including health benefits), with some exceptions
3. All allowances received from an employer for living and work expenses, with some exceptions

There are a few deductions that are available to reduce employment income, and we'll talk about them in a bit. Employment income follows cash basis accounting like we discussed before, so it's based on when you get the money.

What can be considered compensation is pretty straightforward most of the time. The salary, wage, or commission structure is generally outlined in your employment paperwork. Tips are calculated at each tipping event depending on the job you have.

The benefits are what cause s some confusion. People tend to underestimate which of the benefits that they receive are taxable. Here's a list of the common ones:

- Personal use of an employer's car
- Employer provided housing, free or at reduced rents (except in remote areas)
- Cash or cash like gifts, and non cash gifts worth over $500
- Holiday trips and other prizes
- Medical insurance premiums and group life insurance
- Interest free and low interest loans
- Reimbursements for daycare, if not on the premises
- Fitness memberships
- Some moving allowances
- Public transit passes provided

In general, if your employer provides it and you like it, it'll probably show up on your T4 (a tax form) as a taxable benefit.

You can also get non taxable or tax deferred benefits too! The biggest tax deferred ones being any employer-contributed amounts to your RRSP, Registered Pension Plan (RPP), or Pooled Registered Pension Plan (PRPP). You may or may not have one or all of these things, depending on how awesome your employer is. Check with your HR department to be sure. Premiums paid for many insurance types are not taxable, so are any employer provided scholarships or free tuition. If you're interested in the full list of items that are not taxable take a look at this publication[44].

Deductions

Now that we've figured out what goes into your employment income total, let's go about reducing it. There are only 8 categories of items that can be deducted from employment income according to Canadian tax rules.

1. Legal fees paid to collect salary or wages owed to you by an employer
2. Professional membership dues if you are a member of a profession that has them
3. Union dues paid to a trade union
4. Expenses for commissioned employees
5. Travel expenses, if required by the job, and the employee has to pay their own way without being reimbursed
6. Cost of supplies used up in the employment process, if the employee is required to pay for them
7. Contributions to an employer's Registered Pension Plan
8. Office rental or home office expenses, sometimes

Let's go through a quick example to see how employment income is calculated.

Wei is a marketing manager at a large global company. She is paid an annual salary of $60,000 and will receive a performance bonus of $10,000 (to be paid in two installments on December 15 and on January 15). During the year, Wei got the following benefits from her company:

- Pension plan contributions of $5,000Private
- Tennis club membership valued at $1,000. Many of her clients are members and she only visits for client meetings
- A necklace costing $450 as her ten year service award

During the year, Wei made the following payments:

- Contributions to company Registered Pension Plan of $5,000
- Charity donations of $250
- Income tax withholdings of $9,000

- $1,000 for work related supplies her employer required her to purchase at her own expense, that were used up in the year

What's Wei's employment related income for the year?

Income:

Salary	$60,000
First half of bonus	$5,000
Total employment income	**$65,000**

Deductions:

Contributions to company Pension Plan	$5,000
Work related supplies consumed in the year	$1,000
Net Income from Employment	**$59,000**

I left quite a bit out, didn't I? Let's explain. The second half of her bonus will be included in the next year's income due to cash basis accounting. Employer's pension plan contributions are a specifically excluded benefit for tax purposes. The ten year service award is excluded because it's a service award for a period longer than five years and its value is under $500. The golf membership is also excluded since it benefits her employer. Donations are a tax credit, not a deduction. You'll see them later on. Got all that? Let's keep going.

Capital Income

Capital gains or losses are the product of selling assets that were bought to produce long term personal or financial benefits. In theory, you won't be buying and selling these properties very often. As a result, they get a light taxation touch compared to other types of income.

For items that have financial benefits, you have to make sure your intent when buying the property was for long term benefit so that you can get the benefit of having a transaction be classified as capital instead of business income. Whether the asset fulfills those intentions is not up to you, but up to future events. When you sell the asset, you only need to prove its original intent. However, if you make the same type of capital transaction often or own the assets for a short time it could be seen as business income. House flipping is a good example of that scenario.

There are two main types of property that capital gains or losses could apply to, with a third reserved for collectors of very specific items that we won't talk about.

Personal Use Property (PUP): Assets that are used primarily for personal benefit and use that generally don't create financial gains. Examples of PUP are your house, car, boat, land, and large furniture.

Financial Property: Assets whose sole purpose is to generate monetary gains. These include stocks, bonds, buildings, land, equipment, and licenses.

When you sell a capital item the amount you receive, less the item's cost and any expenses to sell, is called the capital gain or capital loss. For tax purposes, only half of that amount is counted, called the Taxable Capital Gain or Allowable Capital Loss. At the end of the year, the two amounts are netted out and included in your income calculation.

If you don't have any Taxable Capital Gains to offset an Allowable Capital Losses in any particular year, good news! They can be carried backwards for 3 tax years and carried forward indefinitely to offset past or future gains.

For personal use property, any losses you experience are deemed to be zero and any gains are taxed. To be even more restrictive, in any given transaction the minimum sales proceeds and minimum cost are both set to $1,000, so small items will have no gain or loss. Each PUP item stands alone for tax purposes, you're not allowed to offset any losses or gains from different PUPs against each other.

Special Cases

Allowable Business Investment losses: For those who invest in small businesses, this allows for the Allowable Capital Loss on the sale or default of the shares of a Canadian Private Company to be used against all sources of income. Otherwise you would only be able to offset it against your Taxable Capital Gains. There are some restrictions to how the underlying company used its assets before you sell it, but it's still a great provision that reduces some of the risk associated with investing in start up businesses.

Lifetime Capital Gains Exemption: You may also be able to avoid any taxes on some capital gains. If you sold shares in the same type of Canadian Private Company above, you will be able to get $835,716 (2017 amount) tax free. The type of company is somewhat restricted, and there are some nitty gritty small details on how to calculate the total amount you get for free. Regardless, this is an amazing tool for entrepreneurs to get value out of their creations tax free.

Superficial Losses: Some geniuses long ago thought that they could create capital losses by selling assets that had lost value, and then buying them back again. The CRA is not okay with that. If any assets are reacquired within 30 days of a previous sale that resulted in a capital loss, that capital loss is denied and retained for the permanent sale of the item later on. It's not gone, but it's delayed. So be careful when you sell any investments.

Principal Residence Exemption: This is the reason so many people use their homes as investments, because it's tax free (most of the time)! Any capital gains you have from selling your primary residence (where you actually live), will be reduced by the following formula:

$$\frac{1 + \text{Number of years as principal residence}}{\text{Number of years you've owned it}} \text{ X Gain}$$

Amazing isn't it? This formula means that if you only have one property and lived in it the entire time you owned it, the entire gain will be tax free. If you have two real estate properties, you will need to assign each year of ownership to one of the properties. If the property was a rental, there are some extra hoops, but it's still possible to get at least some of the gain tax free.

It's example time! Let's suppose you're a boss that has a lot of investments and you sold the following investments in the year:

Property	Selling Price	Cost and Selling Costs	Gain or Loss
Company A Shares	$80,000	$60,000	$20,000
Company B Shares	$20,000	$25,000	($5,000)
House	$750,000	$755,000	($5,000)
Shares of a Private Canadian Company (the special one that qualifies for fun tax benefits)	$10,000	$20,000	($10,000)

What's the capital gain or loss that gets added to your income in this case? $5,000 capital gains which turns into $2,500 taxable capital gains. Did you think it would be $0? The personal property sale of the house doesn't count since losses on PUP are not allowed for tax purposes.

Property Income

Property income is passive income. It's money that you receive on invested capital that you took no time, effort, or work to get (after making the initial capital or time investment). This is not the income from the sale of these investments, just the income they continually give out to their owner while owned.

The main categories of this type of income are: dividends (where stocks pay out money to their owners), interest (from debt of some sort that is owned by an individual), rental income (from real estate or capital asset ownership which can be quite involved if you're a landlord), and royalty income (ownership of intangible property like a patent).

Most property income is measured on an accrual basis. This means that regardless of when money changes hands, if the action to earn or lose it occurs, it also happened for tax purposes. January to December taxation years apply here too.

Each of the four income types is dealt with quite differently tax-wise so let's break them down individually.

Interest Income

The CRA lets an individual to choose from two different methods of accounting for interest income, with an overarching limitation.

The Receivable Method works in the general accrual basis way: as soon as interest payments are announced, you include them in your income regardless of whether they've been paid out or not. The Cash Method is equally as obvious, you only include interest in your income once you've received the cash. Given the choice, most people would probably choose to push the taxes into the future using the Cash Method. That's why the CRA came up with the limitation called the Anniversary Day Accrual Method, which requires you to recognize some income for every 12 month period since the investment's starting date. This usually comes into effect when there are multi-year loans that only pay interest at the end.

Once you've chosen a method of accounting for your interest income, you have to keep that method for the rest of that investment's life. However, you can choose to account for different investments in different ways.

Foreign interest will be reported in Canadian dollars. If there are any taxes withheld by the issuing country, they need to be added back for the Canadian tax calculation, but can be used to reduce the taxes paid as a deduction.

Deductions

Interest on a loan is deductible if the money was used to acquire investment assets that generate revenue. Meaning any mortgage interest would be deductible from your rental income, if you took out a mortgage to buy a rental property. This also extends to taking out loans to buy bonds or stock (although that's highly risky, but you do you).

You can also deduct investment consultant fees, some costs associated with obtaining loans (legal fees, appraisal fees for real estate), management fees for investment portfolios, and accounting costs for determining this income and keeping records.

The interesting thing here is you can have a loss from property income if expenses are higher than your income. However, you may get challenged regarding whether you ever met the 'expectation of profit' test we discussed above.

Dividend Income

Dividend income is calculated on a cash basis, only to be included when received. Even then, it's still one weird calculation.

Canadian Public Company dividends (Eligible Dividends) are included in income at 138% of their distributed value. Canadian Private Company dividends (Non Eligible Dividends) are included in income at 118% of their paid out value. This is called a gross up, and it's done this way to reflect the taxes the companies paid on the income before it was distributed . You then apply your individual marginal tax rate to this amount.

The good news is that you also get tax credit to make up for that initial gross up. Depending on your province, it more or less wipes out the gross up.

If you receive foreign dividends, you don't have to use the gross up math at all. The treatment is the same as foreign interest income. You would report the dividend at the full amount, prior to withholding taxes, in the year it was received. Then you could also potentially claim the withholding tax against your income.

Rental Income

Like business income and many others, rental income is included in your income tax calculations as it is earned, regardless of when you receive it. This is good for landlords who collect the first and last month's rent on a lease agreement, since you won't have to recognize that last month's rent until you are owed it. It also has drawbacks if your tenants aren't paying on time though.

Deductions

Sometimes it's good to be a landlord, it's the most deduction happy area of property income.

You can deduct:
- Interest expenses on the mortgage you used to buy the rent-producing asset
- Costs of obtaining the loan (legal, appraisal, mortgage costs)
- Property taxes
- Landscaping, utilities, insurance
- Repairs and maintenance expenses that are not long term additions
- Property maintenance salaries or fees
- Accounting and record keeping costs
- Any costs incurred to collect on rent (court and legal fees)
- Depreciation

Like with interest income, you can have a loss from rental income if expenses are higher than your income. Some people try to have the tenants pay their mortgage but also not create rental income so they can reduce their taxes even further. The reasonable expectation of profit guideline applies in cases like these and eliminates that possibility. More on that in the business section ahead.

Royalty Income

Royalty income is the simplest of them all. You include it as you earn it. Royalty income can be a result of patents, trademarks, licenses, and other intellectual property you may own.

However, if your royalty income came from a somewhat labourious process, like writing a book or composing music, you may be required to treat this activity as business income instead of royalty income. This will allow you to deduct more items from this income, so you may come out ahead.

Before we move on to the last type of income, let's go through some examples for property income. Jonathan is our new friend who has $1,000,000 from an inheritance to invest. He lives in Ontario. His options are: (a) a bond that pays 10% interest, (b) common shares of a public corporation with a dividend payout ratio of 4%, and (c) a residential property that pays out 8% in rents (after all expenses). We're going to take a look at how each of these investments behave come tax time if he spent the entire amount on each, held them all for one year, and is in the 40% tax bracket.

The interest will be treated as normal income, fully taxable at the 40% tax rate. That $100,000 of income pre-tax will turn into $60,000 after tax ($100,000 x 40%=$40,000 in taxes paid).

Dividends are a little different. $40,000 will be the cash Jonathan received, but since public companies issue eligible dividends, he'll include $55,200 in his income (gross up of 138%). Jonathan will have to pay $8,791 on but gets to reduce this by $13,811 though (credit of 25.02%), so Jonathan's total tax bill is $0. If this is your only income you ain't paying any taxes.

Rental income totaling $80,000 will be treated the same as interest, fully taxable at Jonathan's 40% tax rate. After taxes, that leaves Jonathan with $48,000.

Business Income

Business income is a pretty diverse thing, applying to both individuals and corporations. We're only going to talk about individuals here though, because corporate taxation would take up a whole book. If you're starting a corporation, that's cool, but it's not what this book is about.

As an individual, you earn business income whenever you do something with the expectation of profit in the short term. Mowing lawns, flipping houses or used goods, tutoring, etc.

A business is taxed on its profit: its income less any allowed deductions. Unlike employment income, business income is measured on an accrual basis. This means that regardless of when money changes hands, if the action to earn or lose any of it occurs, it also happened for tax purposes.

Remember when I said an individual's taxation year is January 1–December 31 of any given calendar year? Well, businesses that are not incorporated and run by an individual (a sole proprietorship) must stick to this too. Incorporated businesses can choose whatever dates they please as their taxation year.

Deductions

The CRA has a general rule when it comes to what you're allowed to deduct from your personal business income. Did you incur the expense to create, increase, or maintain revenues? If not, good luck justifying it to the CRA.

Other than straightforward businesses, there's also a rule about activities that generate revenue, but not enough to offset the expenses that come along with them. These are generally hobbyist activities, like painting, being a professional gamer, or being a vlogger. In these cases, the expenses are only deductible as far as the revenue itself goes, down to $0. You won't be allowed to take a loss to reduce any other income you might have because your garage full of organic glitter body soaps hasn't been selling for three years. This is called the 'expectation of profit' guideline, since the CRA expects you to make a profit on these activities and so won't let you deduct expenses for a loss unless you fully intend to make money.

When deducting capital purchases like cars or buildings, the CRA has blanket rules for dealing with these. It's mathy and long-winded, so if you need it you can find it here[45].

On top of all these other rules, there is also a reasonableness test. If the expense passes all these other rules, but is deemed unreasonable in cost, it will be downgraded to a reasonable amount. An example would be hiring family to work for you at exorbitant salaries. You might actually need an employee and the CRA will be okay with that, but if you pay them double market value the CRA will only allow a deduction for the market value salary.

There are also some specifically denied expenses that you may be interested in, but the most useful one is that all food and drink expenses (even if reasonable and for business purposes) are arbitrarily only allowed to be deducted at 50% of their value. Obviously, people abused it and the CRA got mad.

GST/HST

Do you have to collect taxes for the government on top of your prices if you're a small time business? Do you get a rebate of the GST/HST that you've paid on your business expenses?

Most businesses are entitled to a rebate for all GST/HST paid on expenses that would qualify as business expenses. If the expense cannot be deducted, no rebate for you. But you only get the rebate if you charge the tax to your customers.

As for charging customers, you're only required to charge HST/GST if you make more than $30,000 in revenue in a given year. Once you charge and collect these taxes, you must send the full amount to the government. Below this threshold, you don't need to collect or remit it. But you won't get a rebate on your own expenses either.

Other Income and Deductions

This is more of a catch-all category for some very specific items. As a result, each item has its own tax treatment and there is no overall application to this category.

Other Income

The fully taxable items are as follows:

- All withdrawals from Registered Retirement Plans of any kind
- All withdrawals from employer and government pension plans
- Old Age Security received from the Canadian government
- Employment Insurance Plan benefits from the Canadian government
- Income from a Registered Education Savings Plan (RESP)
- Research grant amounts received in excess of the associated research expenses
- Spousal support payments received

Items that are exempt from tax are:

- Scholarships, bursaries, or fellowships received by students (with some caveats)
- Child support payments received

Items that are not taxable at all:

- Lottery or gambling winnings (provided you're not a professional gambler)
- Gifts not related to employment
- Inheritances
- Life insurance payout upon the death of an individual
- Insurance payouts (accidental, medical, home insurance, etc), as long as the premiums were paid at least in part by the individual and not his or her employer

Other Deductions

In the same vein, the deductions section of the other income calculation is also very specific.

The following items can be used to reduce your income:
- Contributions to RRSPs
- Canada Pension Plan contributions if self-employed
- Spousal support payments (by court or written agreement, on a regular schedule)
- Moving expenses for relocating for work or post secondary education (with some restrictions)
- Fees or expenses related to an objection or appeal regarding the Income Tax Act

Tax Advantaged Accounts

We've mentioned the RRSP and TFSA accounts earlier, but I wanted to give you a more detailed look at these accounts and how they can help you put away money for retirement while saving money on your taxes. It's important to start saving money in these accounts early, because there is a limit to how much you can stash in each account per year and you should take advantage of the tax free compounding!

Registered Retirement Savings Plans (RRSPs)

This account allows you to invest with pre-tax dollars, which gives you a much better return over time. Your money will be able to grow, tax-free, until the time it's withdrawn.

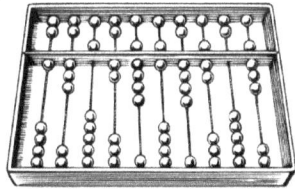

How much money can you put in this vessel of awesome tax deferred riches? 18% of your earned income up to $26,010 (2017 number). Earned income consists of employment income, rental income, royalty income, research grants, and alimony income. If you contribute more than you're allowed to, there's a 1% per month penalty on the extra amounts contributed until they are removed. However, there's $2,000 of leeway for each individual over their lifetime for over contribution which will not be penalized.

If you're not able to contribute in a particular year, don't worry! You'll have the amount available to you in future years. This can be helpful when you're not earning much in your first few years of employment, so you can use the additional room in later years with higher income.

When an employer contributes to an RRSP for you, your RRSP limit is reduced by their contributions. The annual limit is all encompassing, both your contributions and the employer's contributions count towards it.

Money can be withdrawn from an RRSP at anytime with no penalty. It will simply be included in your income as if it was any other type of fully taxable income, like employment or interest incomes. However, there are certain situations where the government will allow you to withdraw funds without including them in income.

Lifelong Learning Plan (LLP): You can withdraw $10,000 per year over a 4 year time period for a full time education or training program for you or your spouse, but the total amount withdrawn cannot exceed $20,000. Any money borrowed has to be paid back into your RRSP over 10 years in equal portions. If not repaid, the amounts will be included in income like regular RRSP withdrawals.

Home Buyer's Plan (HBP): First time homebuyers can withdraw $25,000 from their RRSPs tax free. Any money borrowed must be paid back over 15 years; with any amounts not repaid will simply be included in income as if they were regular RRSP withdrawals.

RRSPs have some considerations as you age. When you turn 71, you must convert the RRSP to a retirement income vehicle of some sort by December 31st of that year. This book is not aimed at retirees so we won't go into the details of choosing between these choices when you retire. If you don't convert the funds into some sort of vehicle, the RRSP will be cancelled the following year and the full amount will be included in your income as taxable.

Tax Free Savings Accounts (TFSAs)

TFSAs are nearly the opposite of RRSP accounts. The income you put into them is after tax (the contributions are not tax deductible), and all the income earned within is absolutely tax free. You read that right.

If you were at least 18 in 2009, you would have $52,000 of TFSA contribution room by December 31, 2017. Annually the contribution amount is around $5,500 per year, occasionally adjusted for inflation or increased depending on the political situation.

In the event of an over contribution, the same penalty applies as it did with the RRSP, 1% per month on any extra money. There is no allowable over contribution with this account. TFSAs have no close out requirement at a certain age either, feel free to leave it to your spouse or dog.

Like with an RRSP, you can take money out of a TFSA at any time. This time there are no tax consequences! What's even better is that the amount you take out will be added back to your contribution room for the next year so you can put it right back if you want to.

For administrative purposes, it's not recommended to contribute to the TFSA after you've withdrawn from it within the same calendar year. The CRA will count it as an over contribution so it's best to wait until the next calendar year to invest if you've taken money out. Plan your contributions and withdrawals accordingly.

RRSP or TFSA?

The majority of the decision depends on where you think your situation is going in terms of tax rates.

Do you think you'll pay more taxes now than in retirement? Then an RRSP is better for you right now. If you're a low earner now and expecting to be in a higher tax bracket later, the TFSA may be better for you. It's also possible that you're suspicious about future tax rates increasing, in which case a TFSA would sooth your soul.

If you have access to RRSPs with an employer match, you should use them up to at least the employer match. It's free money! After that, you should do an evaluation of what is important to you tax-wise. The RRSP has a much higher contribution limit, so if you took the saving section to heart and have a lot to contribute, it's a great way to stash that cash.

You should also consider the types of investments you have available to you in an RRSP versus a TFSA since RRSPs are generally more limited because of the managing companies employers generally choose. If investment options in your RRSP suck, the TFSA might be a smarter move so that you can invest in what your heart really desires (mine desires low cost index funds). Or you could open a self-managed RRSP if you're comfortable with that.

The easiest thing to do is to use all the room you can in both accounts of course. If that's too much, you can split the amounts you have to contribute equally between the plans you have available to you. This approach provides a diversified way to deal with any tax situation the future might bring in case you're wrong about your tax assumptions.

Tax Rates

How much tax do you need to pay on your income? In Canada the tax rates come in two tiers, federal and provincial. Every Canadian resident will be taxed at the federal level, and then again at the provincial level depending on the province they live in.

In Canada we are subject to something called a 'progressive' tax system, which means that the more money you make, the higher the percentage of your income that you pay in taxes. You should understand that due to the progressive system, you are not taxed on your whole income at one rate. Each level of income is taxed at its own rate according to the chart below. This is important to understand if someone has ever told you that a raise or bonus wasn't worth it because you'd end up taking home less money. That's just ridiculously untrue, since only the new money will be taxed at the higher rate.

Your marginal tax rate is the rate of tax applicable on the next dollar you earn. If you already earn $45,916 and are considering a second job, how much of that additional income will you see after taxes? According to the chart below, anything above the $45,916 will be taxed at 20.5% at the federal level which is now your marginal rate.

Your average tax rate is the rate you pay over your entire income for the year, weighted for the amount of income you have in each bracket. It's easily calculated by dividing your tax bill by your income. If we use the same example from above and say you earned an additional $5,000, your average federal tax rate would be 15.54% ($7,912 in taxes paid on $50,916 in income).

The actual brackets and rates may change year over year depending on political things but as of January 2017 the federal tax brackets and rates are as follows[46]:

Income Tax Rate	Income Bracket	Taxes Owed
15%	$0 to $45,916	15% of Taxable Income
20.5%	$45,916 to $91,831	$6,887.40 plus 20.5% of the excess over $45,916
26%	$91,831 to $142,353	$16,299.98,plus 26% of the excess over $91,831
29%	$142,353 to $202,800	$29,435.70 plus 29% of the excess over $142,353
33%	Over $202,800	$33,829.61 plus 33% of the excess over $202,800

The provincial tax rates are added on top of the federal rates. To find the tax rates that apply in your province, you can go here[47]. I would list them all out, but it would take several pages and no one would read it.

Let's do some examples with a few people from different provinces at different income levels. Let's go with Ontario and British Columbia, and then add Alberta to the mix since their brackets are unusual. The full math is in the free content files on my website[48].

The following examples do not include any tax deductions or credits, so they will be higher than the taxes you'll pay in real life. Read up on these in the next section.

Ontario

Income	$40,000	$75,000	$150,000
Total Taxes Paid	$8,131	$17,982	$44,967
Total After Tax Income	$31,869	$57,018	$105,033

British Columbia

Income	$40,000	$75,000	$150,000
Total Taxes Paid	$8,053	$17,598	$46,285
Total After Tax Income	$31,947	$57,402	$103,715

Alberta

Income	$40,000	$75,000	$150,000
Total Taxes Paid	$10,000	$20,350	$47,121
Total After Tax Income	$30,000	$54,650	$102,879

Federal Tax Credits

What we've calculated just now was the full amount of tax you would pay without any credits from the government. Luckily for us, there's quite a few of those that affect a variety of people.

Tax credits reduce taxes owed by a specified amount and are unrelated to your tax rate. The amount of benefit that you'd receive from a credit will always be constant. This is very different from a tax deduction, which reduces your income and will only save you as much money as the difference between the two tax rates between incomes. Tax credits benefit all equally, tax deductions benefit those in the highest tax brackets the most.

Some of the federal tax credits are listed below. The provincial credits vary widely so look to your province's tax website for details.

Refundable Tax Credits are subtracted from the taxes you owe, and allow taxes owed to go below zero into the refund zone. These credits act like direct payments to the CRA. There are not too many of those unfortunately.

Non-Refundable Tax Credits are also subtracted from the taxes you owe, but only till you get to $0. After that, they don't do you any good and don't create a refund, hence the name.

Basic Tax Credit: Every person that files taxes receives $1,745. This is also known as the 'first $10,000 is free' guideline. Basically this credit allows you to earn your first $11,635with no taxes. The credit is calculated at the 15% tax rate which is the lowest rate.

Employment Credit: If you're employed, you get to take $177 off your taxes ($1,177 x 15%). Thanks government!

CPP and EI: You can claim 15% of your maximum allowable CPP and EI contributions in any year. Your tax statements from work will have these amounts on them.

Interest on Student Loans: Now we're talking. You're allowed to deduct 15% of the interest on your student loan payments under the Canada Student Loan Program and provincial student loan programs. This applies to interest only, so it will require some math on your part to figure out how much you paid.

You may use this credit in the year you paid the interest or carry it forward up to 5 years.

Education, Tuition, and Textbooks: This credit has been eliminated in 2017, but if you've gone through schooling prior to 2017 you may still be able to use the information below. Students at a university, college, or other certified post secondary institution are allowed a credit of 15% of tuition costs paid. This is especially great if you went or go to a very expensive institution. On top of that, you can also claim 15% of $464 for each month you are a full time student. Part time students are allowed to claim 15% of $140. These credits can be carried forward indefinitely until you have enough income to use them up. After you've reduced your own taxes to $0, these credits can be transferred to a parent, grandparent, or spouse at a maximum of $750 annually (5,000 x 15%).

First Time Homebuyer's Credit: If you are a first time home buyer, you can take $750 ($5,000 x 15%) off your taxes in that tax year. You cannot have owned a house within the past four years in order to claim this credit.

Charitable Donations: On the first $200 you give to charity, you'll get to take 15% of the amount donated off your taxes. For any amounts over $200, you can deduct 29% of the donation from your taxes. But you can't donate more than 75% of your income in any given year; the excess will be carried forward for 5 years.

Foreign Tax Credit: As discussed before in the investment income section, you may be taxed on foreign income at the source. You are able to deduct those taxes from your income up to the amount that the taxes would be by Canadian standards and then further limited to 15% of the foreign income earned. Any unused balances can be used as a tax deduction.

Illegal Income

So you're a drug dealer, prostitute, or a thief. You're a criminal! Why would you pay taxes? Well, the CRA wants a piece of your business regardless of its legality. It's best to stay ahead of the CRA on this one, because if you ever get caught the taxes will be much higher than they would've been if you had reported your income. And if you don't have the money to pay them, you'll get into even more legal trouble.

In the event that you are caught, after all the legal stuff, your business will be assessed by the CRA and they'll decide on a certain amount of income for your business. This income may or may not be much higher than what you actually made. It will then be up to you to prove them wrong and show them a lower amount. This would be a little hard to do after all your stuff has been seized by the police.

You don't have to tell the CRA that your income is illegal, they don't ask. There's a box for 'Other Income'. They just want their cut. You can deduct business expenses from your income like any other business as well (no bribes, though), so that's nice.

Filing Requirements and Payment

When is the deadline to file your taxes and pay the CRA? For most people, it's April 30th of any given year. If you or your spouse have a business, the date is June 15th.

You don't have to file a tax return if no taxes are payable. If you're not sure you're calculating that right, you should file one anyway. There is a penalty if you mistakenly thought you owed no taxes but actually did and didn't file.

The CRA will take a few weeks to assess your return. They can come back on their assessment, or you can ask them to reassess, within the following limits:

1. If intentionally or due to neglect, you made a misrepresentation of any items on your return, the CRA can reassess at any time
2. Otherwise, there is a three year limit from the date of the original (mailed) assessment. You can waive this time limit if it's beneficial for you to be reassessed
3. The CRA can reassess up to ten years back to let you to claim tax deductions or credits you forgot, but only if you ask them to

Employment income taxes and pension-related income taxes should be withheld and remitted to the government by your employer throughout the year. You're not responsible for this part.

Other types of income that are not subject to withholding taxes must instead be paid to the CRA on a quarterly installment basis. This is only required if your taxes owing to the government was more than $3,000 for both the current year and either of the two previous tax years. The installments are due in March, June, September, and December on the 15th. The installment calculations are somewhat complicated and only apply to a few people so we won't go over them here.

Penalties

Now that you know how to calculate your taxes, let's make sure you know what happens when you don't do it properly.

The Income Tax Act has a few penalties that you should know about:

- Not filing an annual tax return: 5% of the unpaid tax for that year, plus 1% each month for up to a year
- Not reporting an income item: 10% of the tax on the unreported item if you do it more than once in a 3 year time period
- Repeatedly not filing an annual tax return: 10% of the unpaid tax on the second unfilled return and all those after it. With an additional 2% monthly penalty for up to 20 months. In the worst case scenario this could be a fine between $10,000 and $25,000, or imprisonment for up to 12 months
- Submitting false or omitting information on purpose: 50% of the tax owing on the amount left out. In the worst case scenario this could be a fine of between 50% and 200% of the tax evaded, or imprisonment of up to 2 years

Don't lie to the CRA! Even your tax preparer can be penalized for misrepresentation up to $100,000 plus their fee.

Software to Use

Before we talk about which software you can use to file your taxes, you should know about the CRA's filing requirements. The CRA uses two protocols to accept returns, NETFILE and EFILE.

NETFILE is the secure service you can use through a tax preparation software like the ones we'll talk about below. The software links up with NETFILE and securely transmits information to the CRA electronically. Most commercially available software is compatible, here's a list if you're interested[49].

EFILE is similar to NETFILE, but the information will be coming to the CRA from authorized service providers, be it an accounting firm or your neighbourhood accountant.

There are so many tax preparation software and services out there, but which is the fairest of them all?

TurboTax

Formerly called QuickTax, if you've ever heard of it. It's apparently Canada's top tax software (if you trust their advertising). This software is available both online and as a CD. The CD version is only compatible with Windows, so Mac users will have to go online. The online version handles only one return at a time, with the CD versions handling multiple returns.

Price

TurboTax Free–very simple returns

TurboTax Basic ($14.99) –simple returns

TurboTax Standard ($19.99) –files up to 8 returns; most people will find this one sophisticated enough

TurboTax Premier ($34.99) –for those with investments and rental properties

Pros

- Step by step guide leads you through your taxes, asking you pertinent questions along the way
- NETFILE certified
- The software can save your information year after year if you're a returning user
- Ability to flag an item to go back to it if you're missing a particular form
- ProReview, where an Intuit (the company that owns TurboTax and Mint) employee will look over your return for any errors

Cons

- Chat help only unless you get the Basic package, at which point you can get help on the phone
- Advertising for add-on services in-software can get annoying

UFile

This software also claims to be the #1 tax prep software in Canada. Seems to be a pretty busy podium. UFile is available both online and as a CD.

Price

UFile Free–simple return or new filer ($20,000 income cap)
$19.99 for 4 returns
$17.95 for individuals, with an option to add a spouse for $10

Pros

- NETFILE certified
- Automatically slots in tax credits for you
- Analyzes the situation across all the returns you're filing for the best refund
- Faster process than TurboTax, 35 minutes versus 45 minutes

Cons

- The questioning process is a bit briefer than TurboTax's
- Slightly more tax know-how required than when using TurboTax
- Support only through email

SimpleTax

The new kid on the block.

Price

Free! Donations accepted but not required.

Pros

- NETFILE certified
- Supports all kinds of tax situations, including investments and rental income
- Step by step walkthrough
- Clean and simple interface

Cons

- So secure that they can't recover your password for you if you forget it
- Online only

Those are some of the more popular options when it comes to filing the returns yourself. You can also go the old-fashioned way and submit your return on paper, which I'll go through a quick example of in a few pages. Hiring an accountant to do it for you is also an option, but unless you have a business or a complicated rental property, it's likely that you'll be just fine doing it yourself with a little effort.

What if you need some help? You could potentially get your return completed for free.

Returns Filed for Free

If you need help filing your return and meet a few criteria, your return could be done for you for free.

The CRA has a Community Volunteer Income Tax Program (CVITP), where communities and organizations within those communities host free clinics teaching tax preparation or have volunteers preparing tax returns for eligible people. Volunteer tax clinics are offered between February and April each year. You can find them in libraries, schools, and other large community organizations. Other locations are listed on the CRA website.

How do you get this free tax help? You need to a have a moderate income and a simple tax situation. What qualifies as a 'moderate' income? According to the CRA that would be: $30,000 or under per individual, $35,000 for an individual with a dependent (plus $2,500 for each additional dependent), and $40,000 per couple (plus $2,500 for each additional dependent). A dependent can be a child or someone who is under your care for a majority of the time like a disabled individual.

The CRA will classify your tax situation as simple if you have no income or if your income comes from the following sources:
- Employment
- Pension
- CPP, disability, EI, and Social Assistance Benefits
- RRSP withdrawals
- Spousal support payments
- Scholarships, fellowships, bursaries or grants
- Interest (under $1,000)

If your tax situation involves any of the following, it is not considered simple by the CRA:
- Self-employment or employment expenses
- Business or rental income and associated expenses
- Capital gains or losses
- You are filing for bankruptcy
- You are completing a tax return for a deceased person

How to File a Simple Tax Return

We've gone over all the details of taxation; now let's do a walkthrough of a simple tax return with some investments to see how it all goes together. I'll be doing the federal and Ontario paper filings since that's where I live. I don't recommend anyone use the old school paper filing way though. It's tedious and prone to human error since you have to calculate every line yourself. One screw up and the whole return is wrong.

Before you start filing your taxes, there are some forms you need to get from your employers and investment companies.

T4 Statement of Remuneration Paid

A T4 is a tax form you get from your employer. The company writes in how much you've made in the year, any benefits received that are taxable, and any contributions they made to your retirement. This statement also shows the CPP and EI taken off your paycheques, as well as the taxes that have been withheld throughout the year.

Some important boxes are:

14 - Income for the year.

16 - Contributions to CPP.

18 - Contributions to EI.

22 - Income tax deducted (how much tax you've already paid).

42- Employment commissions (if you get some of your pay through commissions).

44 - Union dues (if the employer pays any union dues for you).

46 - Charitable donations (if you or the employer made charitable donations on your behalf through your paycheque).

More information on all available boxes can be found on the CRA website[50]. The items in the lower box of the T4 slip are for CRA use only. Box 40 means other taxable allowances and benefits. Below, you'll find a mock T4 I created for myself to help with this walkthrough.

Employer's name – Nom de l'employeur		Canada Revenue Agency	Agence du revenu du Canada	Year Année	2016		T4 Statement of Remuneration Paid État de la rémunération payée

Awesome Inc.

	Employment income – line 101 Revenus d'emploi – ligne 101	Income tax deducted – line 437 Impôt sur le revenu retenu – ligne 437
14	22	
	60,000 00	9,000 00

54	Employer's account number / Numéro de compte de l'employeur		Province of employment Province d'emploi	Employee's CPP contributions – line 308 Cotisations de l'employé au RPC – ligne 308	EI insurable earnings Gains assurables d'AE
		10		16 3,000 00	24 50,000 00

Social insurance number Numéro d'assurance sociale	Exempt – Exemption CPP/QPP EI PPIP		Employment code Code d'emploi	Employee's QPP contributions – line 308 Cotisations de l'employé au RRQ – ligne 308	CPP/QPP pensionable earnings Gains ouvrant droit à pension – RPC/RRQ
12	28		29	17 00	26 60,000 00
	RPC/RRQ AE RPAP				

Employee's name and address – Nom et adresse de l'employé			Employee's EI premiums – line 312 Cotisations de l'employé à l'AE – ligne 312	Union dues – line 212 Cotisations syndicales – ligne 212
Last name (in capital letters) – Nom de famille (en lettres moulées)	First name – Prénom	Initial – Initiale	18 1,000 00	44

Botvinnik   Victoria

	RPP contributions – line 207 Cotisations à un RPA – ligne 207	Charitable donations – line 349 Dons de bienfaisance – ligne 349
111 Magnificent Lane | 20 2,000 00 | 46 |

	Pension adjustment – line 206 Facteur d'équivalence – ligne 206	RPP or DPSP registration number N° d'agrément d'un RPA ou d'un RPDB
Somewhere Warm, ON | 52 3,000 00 | 50 XXXXX |
A1B 2C3 | | |

	Employee's PPIP premiums – see over Cotisations de l'employé au RPAP – voir au verso	PPIP insurable earnings Gains assurables du RPAP
	55	56

Other information (see over)	Box – Case	Amount – Montant	Box – Case	Amount – Montant	Box – Case	Amount – Montant
	40	1,500 00				

Autres renseignements (voir au verso)	Box – Case	Amount – Montant	Box – Case	Amount – Montant	Box – Case	Amount – Montant

T5 Statement of Investment Income

Next comes the T5, which shows your income from investments for the year. Each financial institution that you hold investments with will send you a separate slip, so you have to diligently track each slip and make sure you have all your information before you sit down to file.

Some important boxes are:

10 to 12 - Non Eligible Dividends (these are generally dividends from private companies).

13 to 17 - Interest (each box number denotes a different type of interest income).

24 to 26 - Eligible Dividends (these are dividends paid out from large generally public companies).

More information on all the available boxes can be found on the CRA website[51]. Here are some mock T5s I created for myself.

T5 Statement of Investment Income / État des revenus de placement — Year/Année 2016

Interest from Canadian sources: 1,500.00
Recipient identification number: XXX-XXX-XXX

Recipient's name and address / Nom, prénom et adresse du bénéficiaire:
Botvinnik, Victoria
111 Magnificent Lane
Somewhere Warm, ON
A1B 2C3

Payer's name and address / Nom et adresse du payeur:
Bonds Galore Inc.

T5 Statement of Investment Income / État des revenus de placement — Year/Année

Actual amount of eligible dividends: 1,000.00
Taxable amount of eligible dividends: 1,380.00
Dividend tax credit for eligible dividends: 207.3

Recipient's name and address / Nom, prénom et adresse du bénéficiaire:
Botvinnik, Victoria
111 Magnificent Lane
Somewhere Warm, ON
A1B 2C3

Payer's name and address / Nom et adresse du payeur:
StockMagic Inc.

If you have investment income, you'll need to fill out an extra form called a Schedule 4. I've filled one out below. It'll flow into your normal tax return form.

T1-2016 Statement of Investment Income *Schedule 4*

State the names of the payers below, and attach any information slips you received. Attach a separate sheet of paper if you need more space. **Attach a copy of this schedule to your return.**

I – Taxable amount of dividends (eligible and other than eligible) from taxable Canadian corporations

Taxable amount of dividends **other than eligible dividends** (specify):		1
	+	2
	+	3
Add lines 1 to 3, and enter this amount on line 180 of your return.	180 =	4
Taxable amount of **eligible dividends** (specify): StockMagic Inc.	+ 1,380 00	5
	+	6
	+	7
Add lines 4 to 7, and enter this amount on line 120 of your return.	120 = 1,380 00	8

II – Interest and other investment income

Specify:	1,500 00	9
	+	10
Income from foreign sources (specify):	+	11
Add lines 9 to 11. Enter this amount on line 121 of your return.	121 = 1,500 00	12

III – Carrying charges and interest expenses

Carrying charges (specify):		13
Interest expenses (specify):	+	14
Add lines 13 and 14. Enter this amount on line 221 of your return.	221 =	15

See the privacy notice on your return.
5000-S4

T1 General Tax Return Form

The OG of tax forms. It's the main one you'll be filling out and everything comes together into this one form. Let's get started!

On the first page you provide the CRA with basic information about yourself that may be useful to the tax process. Marital status is very important to tax filing because married couples have extra benefits and such.

Protected B when completed

T1 GENERAL 2016

Canada Revenue Agency / Agence du revenu du Canada

Income Tax and Benefit Return

Step 1 – Identification and other information

ON 8

Identification

Print your name and address below.

First name and initial
Victoria

Last name
Botvinnik

Mailing address: Apt No – Street No Street name
111 Magnificent Lane

PO Box	RR

City	Prov./Terr	Postal code
Somewhere Warm	ON	A 1 B 2 C 3

Email address

I understand that by providing an email address, I am registering for online mail. I have read and I accept the terms and conditions on page 17 of the guide.

Enter an email address.

Information about your residence

Enter your province or territory of residence on **December 31, 2016**: Ontario

Enter the province or territory where you **currently** reside if it is not the same as your mailing address above.

If you were self-employed in 2016, enter the province or territory of self-employment.

If you **became** or **ceased** to be a resident of Canada for income tax purposes in 2016, enter the date of:

	Month Day			Month Day
entry		or	departure	

Information about you

Enter your social insurance number (SIN): X X X X X X X X X

Enter your date of birth: Year Month Day

Your language of correspondence
Votre langue de correspondance: English ✓ Français

Is this return for a deceased person?

If this return is for a **deceased** person, enter the date of death: Year Month Day

Marital status

Tick the box that applies to your marital status on December 31, 2016:

1 ☐ Married   2 ☐ Living common-law   3 ☐ Widowed
4 ☐ Divorced   5 ☐ Separated   6 ☑ Single

Information about your spouse or common-law partner (if you ticked box 1 or 2 above)

Enter his or her SIN:

Enter his or her first name:

Enter his or her net income for 2016 to claim certain credits:

Enter the amount of universal child care benefit (UCCB) from line 117 of his or her return:

Enter the amount of UCCB repayment from line 213 of his or her return:

Tick this box if he or she was self-employed in 2016   1 ☐

Do not use this area

Elections Canada (For more information, see page 19 in the guide.)

A) Do you have Canadian citizenship? .... Yes ☑ 1 No ☐ 2

Answer the following question only if you have Canadian citizenship.

B) As a Canadian citizen, do you authorize the Canada Revenue Agency to give your name, address, date of birth, and citizenship to Elections Canada to update the National Register of Electors? ...... Yes ☑ 1 No ☐ 2

Your authorization is valid until you file your next tax return. Your information will only be used for purposes permitted under the *Canada Elections Act*, which include sharing the information with provincial/territorial election agencies, members of Parliament, registered political parties, and candidates at election time.

Do not use this area	172				171			

5006-R

Next up is a nice summary of your T4 and T5 information. Be careful when adding up all those numbers! That's why tax preparation software does all the math for you.

194

Step 1 – Identification and other information (continued)

Please answer the following question:

Did you own or hold specified foreign property where the total cost amount of all such property,
at any time in 2016, was more than CAN$100,000?
See "Specified foreign property" in the guide for more information. . . . . 266 Yes ☐ 1   No ☑ 2

If **yes**, complete Form T1135 and attach it to your return.
If you had dealings with a non-resident trust or corporation in 2016, see "Other foreign property" in the guide.

Step 2 – Total income

As a resident of Canada, you have to report your income from all sources both inside and outside Canada.
When you come to a line on the return that applies to you, go to the line number in the guide for more information.

Employment income (box 14 of all T4 slips)			101	60,000 00
Commissions included on line 101 (box 42 of all T4 slips)	102			
Wage loss replacement contributions (see line 101 in the guide)	103			
Other employment income			104 +	
Old age security pension (box 18 of the T4A(OAS) slip)			113 +	
CPP or QPP benefits (box 20 of the T4A(P) slip)			114 +	
Disability benefits included on line 114 (box 16 of the T4A(P) slip)	152			
Other pensions and superannuation			115 +	
Elected split-pension amount (**attach** Form T1032)			116 +	
Universal child care benefit (UCCB)			117 +	
UCCB amount designated to a dependant	185			
Employment insurance and other benefits (box 14 of the T4E slip)			119 +	
Taxable amount of dividends (eligible **and** other than eligible) from taxable Canadian corporations (**attach** Schedule 4)			120 +	1,380 00
Taxable amount of dividends other than eligible dividends, included on line 120, from taxable Canadian corporations	180			
Interest and other investment income (**attach** Schedule 4)			121 +	1,500 00
Net partnership income: limited or non-active partners only			122 +	
Registered disability savings plan income			125 +	
Rental income Gross 160		Net 126 +		
Taxable capital gains (**attach** Schedule 3)			127 +	
Support payments received Total 156		Taxable amount 128 +		
RRSP income (from all T4RSP slips)			129 +	
Other income Specify:			130 +	
Self employment income				
Business income Gross 162		Net 135 +		
Professional income Gross 164		Net 137 +		
Commission income Gross 166		Net 139 +		
Farming income Gross 168		Net 141 +		
Fishing income Gross 170		Net 143 +		
Workers' compensation benefits (box 10 of the T5007 slip)	144			
Social assistance payments	145 +			
Net federal supplements (box 21 of the T4A(OAS) slip)	146 +			
Add lines 144, 145, and 146 (see line 250 in the guide).	=	▶ 147 +		
Add lines 101, 104 to 143, and 147.	This is your total income. 150 =			62,880 00

5000-R

Protected B when completed **3**

Attach only the documents (schedules, information slips, forms, or receipts) **requested in the guide** to support any claim or deduction. Keep all other supporting documents.

Step 3 – Net income

Enter your **total income** from line 150			150	62,880 00
Pension adjustment (box 52 of all T4 slips and box 034 of all T4A slips)	**206**	3,000 00		
Registered pension plan deduction (box 20 of all T4 slips and box 032 of all T4A slips)	**207**	2,000 00		
RRSP/pooled registered pension plan (PRPP) deduction (see Schedule 7 and **attach** receipts)			**208** +	
PRPP **employer** contributions (amount from your PRPP contribution receipts)	**205**			
Deduction for elected split-pension amount (**attach** Form T1032)			**210** +	
Annual union, professional, or like dues (box 44 of all T4 slips, and receipts)			**212** +	
Universal child care benefit repayment (box 12 of all RC62 slips)			**213** +	
Child care expenses (**attach** Form T778)			**214** +	
Disability supports deduction			**215** +	
Business investment loss Gross **228**		Allowable deduction **217** +		
Moving expenses			**219** +	
Support payments made Total **230**		Allowable deduction **220** +		
Carrying charges and interest expenses (**attach** Schedule 4)			**221** +	
Deduction for CPP or QPP contributions on self-employment and other earnings (**attach** Schedule 8 or Form RC381, whichever applies)			**222** +	·
Exploration and development expenses (**attach** Form T1229)			**224** +	
Other employment expenses			**229** +	
Clergy residence deduction			**231** +	
Other deductions Specify:			**232** +	
Add lines 207, 208, 210 to 224, 229, 231, and 232.			**233** = 2,000 00 ▶	– 2,000 00
Line 150 minus line 233 (if negative, enter "0")		This is your **net income before adjustments**.	**234** =	60,880 00
Social benefits repayment (if you reported income on line 113, 119, or 146, see line 235 in the guide) Use the federal worksheet to calculate your repayment.			**235** –	·
Line 234 minus line 235 (if negative, enter "0") If you have a spouse or common-law partner, see line 236 in the guide.		This is your net income.	**236** =	60,880 00

Step 4 – Taxable income

Canadian Forces personnel and police deduction (box 43 of all T4 slips)		**244**	
Employee home relocation loan deduction (box 37 of all T4 slips)		**248** +	
Security options deductions		**249** +	
Other payments deduction (if you reported income on line 147, see line 250 in the guide)		**250** +	
Limited partnership losses of other years		**251** +	
Non-capital losses of other years		**252** +	
Net capital losses of other years		**253** +	
Capital gains deduction		**254** +	
Northern residents deductions (**attach** Form T2222)		**255** +	
Additional deductions Specify:		**256** +	
Add lines 244 to 256.		**257** = ▶	–
Line 236 minus line 257 (if negative, enter "0")	This is your taxable income.	**260** =	60,880 00

Step 5 – Federal tax and provincial or territorial tax

Use Schedule 1 to calculate your federal tax and Form 428 to calculate your provincial or territorial tax.

5000-R

This is where the return gets interesting and wants you to add some more schedules. Page 4 of the T1 wants you to calculate your taxes owing both federally and provincially by attaching something called a Schedule 1 for your federal taxes owing and a Form 428 for provincial or territorial taxes. Let's do that before we go back to the T1.

Schedule 1 will walk you through all the federally available tax credits that you could potentially use to lower your taxes payable. It also helps you calculate the amount you owe with a handy chart.

Protected B when completed

T1-2016   Federal Tax   Schedule 1

This is **Step 5** in completing your return. Complete this schedule and **attach** a copy to your return. For more information, see the related line in the guide.

Step 1 – Federal non-refundable tax credits

Basic personal amount	claim $11,474 **300**	11,474 00	1
Age amount (if you were born in 1951 or earlier) (use the federal worksheet)	(maximum $7,125) **301**+		2
Spouse or common-law partner amount (**attach** Schedule 5)	**303**+		3
Amount for an eligible dependant (**attach** Schedule 5)	**305**+		4
Family caregiver amount for infirm children under 18 years of age			
Number of children for whom you **are claiming** the family caregiver amount **352** × $2,121 =	**367**+		5
Amount for infirm dependants age 18 or older (**attach** Schedule 5)	**306**+		6
CPP or QPP contributions: through employment from box 16 and box 17 of all T4 slips (**attach** Schedule 8 or Form RC381, whichever applies)	**308**+	3,000 00	• 7
on self-employment and other earnings (**attach** Schedule 8 or Form RC381, whichever applies)	**310**+		• 8
Employment insurance premiums: through employment from box 18 and box 55 of all T4 slips	(maximum $955.04) **312**+	955 04	• 9
on self-employment and other eligible earnings (**attach** Schedule 13)	**317**+		•10
Volunteer firefighters' amount	**362**+		11
Search and rescue volunteers' amount	**395**+		12
Canada employment amount (If you reported employment income on line 101 or line 104, see line 363 in the guide.) (maximum $1,161)	**363**+	1,161 00	13
Public transit amount	**364**+		14
Children's arts amount	**370**+		15
Home accessibility expenses (**attach** Schedule 12)	**398**+		16
Home buyers' amount	**369**+		17
Adoption expenses	**313**+		18
Pension income amount (use the federal worksheet)	(maximum $2,000) **314**+		19
Caregiver amount (**attach** Schedule 5)	**315**+		20
Disability amount (for self) (claim **$8,001**, or if you were under 18 years of age, use the federal worksheet)	**316**+		21
Disability amount transferred from a dependant (use the federal worksheet)	**318**+		22
Interest paid on your student loans	**319**+		23
Your tuition, education, and textbook amounts (**attach** Schedule 11)	**323**+		24
Tuition, education, and textbook amounts transferred from a child	**324**+		25
Amounts transferred from your spouse or common-law partner (**attach** Schedule 2)	**326**+		26
Medical expenses for **self, spouse or common-law partner, and your dependent children born in 1999 or later** **330**		27	
Enter $2,237 or 3% of line 236 of your return, whichever is **less**. –		28	
Line 27 minus line 28 (if negative, enter "0") =		29	
Allowable amount of medical expenses for **other dependants** (do the calculation at line 331 in the guide) **331**+		30	
Add lines 29 and 30. =	▶ **332**+		31
Add lines 1 to 26, and line 31.	**335**=	16,590 04	32
Federal non-refundable tax credit rate	×	15%	33
Multiply line 32 by line 33.	**338**=	2,488 51	34
Donations and gifts (**attach** Schedule 9)	**349**+		35
Add lines 34 and 35. Enter this amount on line 48 on the next page. Total federal non-refundable tax credits **350**=		2,488 51	36

Continue on the next page.

Protected B when completed

Enter your **taxable income** from line 260 of your return. 60,880 00 **37**

	Line 37 is $45,282 or less	Line 37 is more than $45,282 but not more than $90,563	Line 37 is more than $90,563 but not more than $140,388	Line 37 is more than $140,388 but not more than $200,000	Line 37 is more than $200,000	
Complete the appropriate column depending on the amount on line 37.						
Enter the amount from line 37.		60,880 00				**38**
Line 38 minus line 39 (cannot be negative)	− 0 00 =	− 45,282 00 = 15,598 00	− 90,563 00 =	− 140,388 00 =	− 200,000 00 =	**39** **40**
Multiply line 40 by line 41.	× 15% =	× 20.5% = 3,197 59	× 26% =	× 29% =	× 33% =	**41** **42**
	+ 0 00	+ 6,792 00	+ 16,075 00	+ 29,029 00	+ 46,317 00	**43**
Add lines 42 and 43.	=	= 9,989 59	=	=	=	**44**

Enter the amount from line 44. 9,989 59 **45**
Federal tax on split income (from line 5 of Form T1206) **424**+ •**46**
Add lines 45 and 46. **404** = 9,989 59 ▶ 9,989 59 **47**

Enter your total federal non-refundable tax credits from line 36 on the previous page. **350** 2,488 51 **48**
Federal dividend tax credit **425**+ 150 20 •**49**
Minimum tax carryover (**attach** Form T691) **427**+ •**50**
Add lines 48, 49, and 50. = 2,638 71 ▶ 2,638 71 **51**

Line 47 minus line 51 (if negative, enter "0") **Basic federal tax 429** = 7,350 88 **52**

Federal foreign tax credit (**attach** Form T2209) **405** − **53**

Line 52 minus line 53 (if negative, enter "0") **Federal tax 406** = 7,350 88 **54**

Total federal political contributions (**attach** receipts) **409** 55
Federal political contribution tax credit (use the federal worksheet) (maximum $650) **410** •**56**
Investment tax credit (**attach** Form T2038(IND)) **412**+ •**57**
Labour-sponsored funds tax credit (see lines 413, 414, 411 and 419 in the guide)
Net cost of shares of a federally registered fund **411** Allowable credit **419**+ •**58**
Net cost of shares of a provincially registered fund **413** Allowable credit **414**+ •**59**
Add lines 56 to 59. **416** = ▶ − **60**
Line 54 minus line 60 (if negative, enter "0") If you have an amount on line 46 above, see Form T1206. **417** = 7,350 88 **61**
Working income tax benefit advance payments received (box 10 of the RC210 slip) **415**+ •**62**

Special taxes (see line 418 in the guide) **418** + **63**

Add lines 61, 62, and 63. Enter this amount on line 420 of your return. **Net federal tax 420** = 7,350 88 **64**

See the privacy notice on your return

Form 428 is more or less the same as Schedule 1 but on a provincial or territorial level.

Protected **B** when completed

ON428

Ontario

Ontario Tax

T1 General – 2016

Complete this form and **attach a copy** to your return. For more information, see the related line in the forms book.

Step 1 – Ontario non-refundable tax credits

	For internal use only	5605		
Basic personal amount	claim $10,011	5804	10,011 00	**1**
Age amount (if born in 1951 or earlier) (use the *Provincial Worksheet*)	(maximum $4,888)	5808 +		**2**

Spouse or common-law partner amount

Base amount	9,350 00				
Minus: his or her net income from page 1 of your return	−				
Result: (if negative, enter "0")	=	(maximum $8,500) ▶	5812 +		**3**

Amount for an eligible dependant

Base amount	9,350 00				
Minus: his or her net income from line 236 of his or her return	−				
Result: (if negative, enter "0")	=	(maximum $8,500) ▶	5816 +		**4**

Amount for infirm dependants age 18 or older (use the *Provincial Worksheet*)		5820 +		**5**

CPP or QPP contributions:

(amount from line 308 of your federal Schedule 1)		5824 +	3,000 00	* **6**
(amount from line 310 of your federal Schedule 1)		5828 +		* **7**

Employment insurance premiums:

(amount from line 312 of your federal Schedule 1)		5832 +	955 04	* **8**
(amount from line 317 of your federal Schedule 1)		5829 +		* **9**
Adoption expenses	(maximum $12,214)	5833 +		**10**
Pension income amount	(maximum $1,384)	5836 +		**11**
Caregiver amount (use the *Provincial Worksheet*)		5840 +		**12**

Disability amount (for self) (Claim **$8,088**, or if you were under 18 years of age, use the *Provincial Worksheet*.)	5844 +		**13**
Disability amount transferred from a dependant (use the *Provincial Worksheet*)	5848 +		**14**
Interest paid on your student loans (amount from line 319 of your federal Schedule 1)	5852 +		**15**
Your tuition and education amounts (use and **attach** Schedule ON(S11))	5856 +		**16**
Tuition and education amounts transferred from a child	5860 +		**17**
Amounts transferred from your spouse or common-law partner (use and **attach** Schedule ON(S2))	5864 +		**18**

Medical expenses:

(Read line 5868 in the forms book.)	5868		19	
Enter $2,266 **or** 3% of line 236 of your return, whichever is **less.**		−	20	
Line 19 minus line 20 (if negative, enter "0")		=	21	

Allowable amount of medical expenses for other dependants (use the *Provincial Worksheet*)	5872 +		22	
Add lines 21 and 22.	5876 =		▶ +	23
Add lines 1 to 18, and line 23.		5880 =	13,966 04	24
Ontario non-refundable tax credit rate			× 5.05%	25
Multiply line 24 by line 25.		5884 =	705 29	26

Donations and gifts:

Amount from line 16 of your federal Schedule 9	× 5.05% =		27	
Amount from line 17 of your federal Schedule 9	× 11.16% =	+	28	
Add lines 27 and 28.	5896 =		▶ +	29

Add lines 26 and 29. Enter this amount on line 42.	Ontario non-refundable tax credits	6150 ▶	705 29	30

Continue on the next page.

5006-C

Step 2 – Ontario tax on taxable income

Enter your **taxable income** from line 260 of your return.
If this amount is more than $20,000, you **must** complete **Step 7 – Ontario health premium.** | 60,880 00 | **31**

Complete the appropriate column depending on the amount on line 31.	Line 31 is $41,536 or less		Line 31 is more than $41,536 but not more than $83,075		Line 31 is more than $83,075 but not more than $150,000		Line 31 is more than $150,000 but not more than $220,000		Line 31 is more than $220,000		
Enter the amount from line 31			60,880 00								**32**
Line 32 minus line 33 (cannot be negative)	−	0 00	−	41,536 00	−	83,075 00	−	150,000 00	−	220,000 00	**33**
	=		=	19,344 00	=		=		=		**34**
	×	5.05%	×	9.15%	×	11.16%	×	12.16%	×	13.16%	**35**
Multiply line 34 by line 35.	=		=	1,769 98	=		=		=		**36**
Add lines 36 and 37.	+	0 00	+	2,098 00	+	5,898 00	+	13,367 00	+	21,879 00	**37**
Ontario tax on taxable income	=		=	3,867 98	=		=		=		**38**

Step 3 – Ontario tax

Enter your Ontario tax on taxable income from line 38.		3,867 98	**39**
Enter your Ontario tax on split income from Form T1206.	**6151** +		• **40**
Add lines 39 and 40.	=	3,867 98	**41**
Enter your Ontario non-refundable tax credits from line 30.	−	705 29	**42**
Line 41 minus line 42 (if negative, enter "0").	=	3,162 69	**43**

Ontario minimum tax carryover:

Enter the amount from line 43.	3,162 69	**44**	
Enter your Ontario dividend tax credit from line 6152 of the *Provincial Worksheet.*	− 138 00	**45**	
Line 44 minus line 45 (if negative, enter "0").	= 3,024 69	**46**	
Amount from line 427 of your federal Schedule 1 × 33.67% =		**47**	

Enter the amount from line 46 or 47, whichever is less.	**6154** −		• **48**
Line 43 minus line 48 (if negative, enter "0").	=	3,162 69	**49**

Ontario surtax

Enter the amount from line 49.	3,162 69	**50**	
Enter the amount from line 40.	−	**51**	
Line 50 minus line 51 (if negative, enter "0").	= 3,162 69	**52**	

Complete lines 53 to 55 only if the amount on line 52 is **more than $4,484.**
Otherwise, enter "0" on line 55 and continue completing the form.

(Line 52	minus $4,484) × 20% (if negative, enter "0") =		53	
(Line 52	minus $5,739) × 36% (if negative, enter "0") =	+	54	
Add lines 53 and 54.		= ▶ +		55
Add lines 49 and 55.		=	3,162 69	56

Ontario dividend tax credit:

Enter your Ontario dividend tax credit from line 6152 of the *Provincial Worksheet.*	**6152** −	138 00	• **57**
Line 56 minus line 57 (if negative, enter "0").	=	3,024 69	**58**

Ontario additional tax for minimum tax purposes:

If you entered an amount other than "0" on line 95 of Form T691, enter your Ontario additional tax for
minimum tax purposes from line 59 of the *Provincial Worksheet.* | + | | 59

Add lines 58 and 59.	=	3,024 69	60

Continue on the next page.

5006-C

Enter the amount from line 60 on the previous page.	3,024 69	61

If you are **not** claiming an Ontario tax reduction, there is an amount on line 59, or the amount on line 61 is "0", enter the amount from line 61 on line 69 and continue completing the form. Otherwise, complete lines 62 to 68 to calculate the Ontario tax reduction.

Step 4 – Ontario tax reduction

Basic reduction				231 00	62
If you had a spouse or common-law partner on December 31, 2016, **only** the individual with the **higher net income** can claim the amounts on lines 63 and 64.					
Reduction for dependent children born in 1998 or later					
Number of dependent children 6269	× $427 =	+			63
Reduction for dependants with a mental or physical impairment					
Number of dependants 6097	× $427 =	+			64
Add lines 62, 63, and 64.		=		231 00	65
Enter the amount from line 65.	231 00 × 2 =		462 00		66
Enter the amount from line 61.		−	3,024 69		67
Line 66 minus line 67 (if negative, enter "0")	Ontario tax reduction claimed	=	0	▶ −	0	68
Line 61 minus line 68 (if negative, enter "0")				= 3,024 69	69

Step 5 – Ontario foreign tax credit

Enter the Ontario foreign tax credit from Form T2036.		−	70
Line 69 minus line 70 (if negative, enter "0")		= 3,024 69	71

Step 6 – Community food program donation tax credit for farmers

Enter the amount of qualifying donations that have also been claimed as charitable donations 6098	× 25% =		−	72
Line 71 minus line 72 (if negative, enter "0")			= 3,024 69	73

Step 7 – Ontario health premium

If your taxable income (from line 31) is not more than $20,000, enter "0". Otherwise, enter the amount calculated in the chart on the next page.	Ontario health premium ▶	+ 600 00	74
Add lines 73 and 74. Enter the result on line 428 of your return.	Ontario tax	= 3,625 69	75

Continue on the next page.

5006-C

And that concludes the accessory returns required to find out how much tax you owe at both levels of government. You'll input the amounts you got in Schedule 1 and Form 428 in the main return to figure out your total taxes owing. Then you'll take out the taxes you've already paid throughout the year, plus potentially some other deductions, and voila! You either have a refund or a payable balance.

Step 6 – Refund or balance owing

Net federal tax: enter the amount from line 64 of Schedule 1 (**attach** Schedule 1, even if the result is "0")	420	7,350 88
CPP contributions payable on self-employment and other earnings (**attach** Schedule 8 or Form RC381, whichever applies)	421 +	
Employment insurance premiums payable on self-employment and other eligible earnings (**attach** Schedule 13)	430 +	
Social benefits repayment (amount from line 235)	422 +	
Provincial or territorial tax (**attach** Form 428, even if the result is "0")	428 +	3,625 69
Add lines 420, 421, 430, 422, and 428. This is your total payable	435 =	10,975 57
Total income tax deducted	437	9,000 00
Refundable Quebec abatement	440 +	
CPP overpayment (enter your excess contributions)	448 +	
Employment insurance overpayment (enter your excess contributions)	450 +	44 96
Refundable medical expense supplement (use the federal worksheet)	452 +	
Working income tax benefit (WITB) (**attach** Schedule 6)	453 +	
Refund of investment tax credit (**attach** Form T2038(IND))	454 +	
Part XII.2 trust tax credit (box 38 of all T3 slips)	456 +	
Employee and partner GST/HST rebate (**attach** Form GST370)	457 +	
Children's fitness tax credit Eligible fees 458 × 15% =	459 +	
Eligible educator school supply tax credit Supplies expenses 488 × 15% =	469 +	
Tax **paid** by instalments	476 +	
Provincial or territorial credits (**attach** Form 479 if it applies)	479 +	
Add lines 437 to 479. These are your total credits	482 = 9,044 96	– 9,044 96
Line 435 minus line 482. This is your refund or balance owing		= 1,930 61

If the result is negative, you have a **refund**. If the result is positive, you have a **balance owing**.

Enter the amount below on whichever line applies.

Generally, we do not charge or refund a difference of $2 or less.

Refund 484		Balance owing 485	1,930 61

For more information on how to make your payment, see line 485 in the guide or go to cra.gc.ca/payments. Your payment is due no later than April 30, 2017.

Direct deposit – Enrol or update (see line 484 in the guide)

You do not have to complete this area every year. Do not complete it this year if your direct deposit information has not changed.

To enrol for direct deposit, to update your banking information, or to request that all of your CRA payments you may be receiving or owed be deposited into the same account as your T1 refund, complete lines 460, 461, and 462 below.

By providing my banking information **I authorize** the Receiver General to deposit in the bank account number shown below **any amounts payable** to me by the CRA, until otherwise notified by me. I understand that this authorization will replace all of my previous direct deposit authorizations.

Branch number 460   (5 digits)   Institution number 461   (3 digits)   Account number 462   (maximum 12 digits)

Ontario opportunities fund

You can help reduce Ontario's debt by completing this area to donate some or all of your 2016 refund to the Ontario opportunities fund. Please see the provincial pages for details.

Amount from line 484 above		1
Your donation to the Ontario opportunities fund	465 –	2
Net refund (line 1 minus line 2)	466 =	3

I certify that the information given on this return and in any documents attached is correct and complete and fully discloses all my income.
Sign here
It is a serious offence to make a false return.
Telephone   Date

490 If a fee was charged for preparing this return, complete the following:
Name of preparer:
Telephone:
EFILE number (if applicable): 489

Personal information is collected under the *Income Tax Act* to administer tax, benefits, and related programs. It may also be used for any purpose related to the administration or enforcement of the Act such as audit, compliance and the payment of debts owed to the Crown. It may be shared or verified with other federal, provincial/territorial government institutions to the extent authorized by law. Failure to provide this information may result in interest payable, penalties or other actions. Under the *Privacy Act*, individuals have the right to access their personal information and request correction if there are errors or omissions. Refer to Info Source cra.gc.ca/gncy/tp/nfsrc/nfsrc-eng.html, personal information bank CRA PPU 005.

Do not use this area 487 488   486

5006-R

At this point, you'll mail that paper form in like your grandma would and wait patiently for the refund cheque to arrive, or for the payment cheque to clear. That's pretty much it. That wasn't so hard, was it? It'll be even easier with software that just asks you questions and plugs in all your numbers in for you. Who needs a fancy, expensive accountant?

5 Six Months to Being Awesome With Money

Throughout this book you've learned all the technical knowledge you need in order to lead a financially sound life. But giving you the textbook isn't going to help you. Just having the knowledge won't make you a fantastic saver, or get you out of debt. I theoretically know how to swim, but if I never did much practicing, there's no way I could beat an Olympic swimmer. So let's do some practice! By going through a weekly program that uses everything in this book, I'm going to help you get your financial affairs in order. It's a three hour commitment once per week for 21 weeks (about six months). You can group a few sessions in one day or do a few per week if you're keen. It's all up to you. But by the end of this, money won't be scary anymore.

Week One

Organization is key for a chill attitude towards money. If you lose the keys to your home, do you know if the landlord will give you a free pair or if you have to pay, and how much? Do you know where the lease papers are? Probably in a box somewhere. Do you know when all the credit cards are due? It's on a bill somewhere, but where's the bill? This week, we'll deal with these types of questions. Crank up the music and sniff out every single financially relevant piece of paper or plastic in your home and dump it out on a clean surface.

These include:
- Credit Card bills
- Utility bills
- Lease or mortgage agreement
- Phone bills
- Insurance statements (home insurance or medical)
- Internet bills
- Medical bills

- Car lease and insurance papers
- Retirement accounts statements (from work or your own)
- Every card you have (debit, credit, insurance ID, etc.)
- Every receipt you find

Once all the paper is out there for you to see, you have to figure out your organization structure. You basically have two choices: digital storage or a multiple pocket folder[52]. Personally I use both, in case the physical copies get burned in a fire or stolen, or if Google's servers crash one day for some crazy reason. Having the information online also allows you to look at it on the go if you're a control freak like I am.

If you've chosen a physical organization system, go out and get that folder from an office supply store, they come in a variety of materials and sizes. Get a letter-sized one of a material of your choice, mine's a plastic one, but they do come in sexier leather styles if you're into that aesthetic. Next, you'll need to label the pockets. I recommend the following labels: Home, Utilities, Transportation, Medical, Financial, Savings & Retirement, Work, and Taxes. Leases, mortgage agreements, home or renter's insurance all go under Home. Utility, phone, and internet bills go under Utilities. Your car or public transit documents should go under Transportation. Under Medical, you can put insurance statements and any receipts for items that get reimbursed through insurance or you paid out of pocket for. In Financial, you'll put all credit card bills and anything else that's financial, but not a fixed cost. For Savings & Retirement, you'll put in all the statements you receive from your work or personal retirement accounts (don't worry if these don't exist yet, we'll get to it). In the Work folder, put your employment contract or offer letter, as well as any reimbursable expenses and expense reports that have not been paid out yet. The Taxes folder is for information the CRA sends you and anything you might want to declare or deduct on your taxes. Pay stubs will go here too. If you have older bills that have already been paid and are just sitting around, make sure to shred them since they don't serve a purpose anymore.

Your life is unique, so feel free to add more folders if you have specific expense categories that I haven't covered. Pets usually need veterinary care, so they might need their own folder. If you run a business, it will definitely need a folder or two. This advice is meant as a guideline, customize it to fit your life.

If you're using the internet or a computer to store your documents, scan everything relevant into PDFs. Create folders with the same headings we used above and slot the documents in there in the same way you would if they were paper. You can also put the information on a password-protected USB stick and hide it somewhere if you're into that.

Although not financial in nature, you might also want to keep other important documents in your new organizational system. Passport, birth certificate, immunization records, etc. should be housed in a safe and easily accessible place in case you need them.

Now you're ready to mark due dates into your calendar so you never miss a payment. Take a look through your bills and make a note of all the different due dates for each item. Write them out in a calendar or agenda if you're a paper person or create alerts in a calendar app. Make sure the alerts are set with enough time for payments to clear. If your credit card is due on the 15th of every month, set the 12th as the 'due date' since some online payments take a few days to go through. If you choose to automate your payments, you'll have fewer dates to keep track of!

If you have a job where you have work expenses and are reimbursed for them, you might also want to invest in a mini expandable file folder to separate personal expenses from corporate[53]. It looks like a long wallet, so it won't cramp your style too much. At the end of the day, empty it out into your file folders.

I really hope that only took three hours, but it's possible that it was a bit more than that. It'll get easier!

Some homework: from now on, keep all receipts for every grocery store visit you make. We're going to go over them in a few weeks. If you use credit and debit for your purchases, those are the only receipts I want you to keep. If you use cash, keep all receipts from all purchases. If there are purchases that don't come with receipts, like parking meters, jot them down in your phone or on a piece of paper. We want to have a good amount of information on your purchase history before we start budgeting.

Week Two

Another administrative week! We're taking it slow on purpose, I don't want to intimidate you with budgets and investing early on. Slow and steady wins the race, after all. This week's focus is protecting your assets and identity.

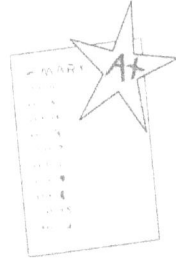

Go online and order your credit report from Equifax or Transunion. The report itself should be free. If you don't foresee needing to get a credit score pulled in the next year, get the full report with a score as well. It's all online and the delivery is instant. Get yourself a cup of your favorite hot (or cold, if it's summer) beverage, and take a long, hard read through every loan you've ever taken out in your life. Is all the information on the report correct? Do you see any loans you didn't take out? These reports can have mistakes if you have a somewhat common name. It's also possible that relatives have taken out loans in your name (it happens). If you see something that you don't think should be there, contact the company who you ordered the report from. If you suspect someone had access to your Social Insurance Number and took out a loan in your name, also put a call in to the police to get that formalized. Regardless of who took out that loan under your name, it's a crime. When you're done taking a look at the report, file it in your folder under Financial.

If you got your score as well, take a look at the number. Is it what you expected? If it's lower, you should try to figure out what happened. Have you missed more payments than you thought you did? Did you forget you had a credit card and stopped using it for more than a year? This will sometimes make the credit card be taken out of your report's calculations as far as 'credit available' volume goes.

Also this week, go around your home and take pictures of expensive items that may need to be claimed for insurance (home or renter's) in the event of theft or damage. Anything that costs over $500 to replace would be something I would care about. If you have receipts or online confirmations from when you bought the items, keep those with the pictures as proof of the item's value.

Further along the protecting yourself route, go through all of your online financial accounts and check the passwords. Are they strong? So many people use easily hackable information like birthdates and pet names, it's ridiculous. Do you really trust that password to stand between a hacker and your future? What if you had a million dollars in that account? In today's world, your online security is only as good as you make it. Use a random password generator to create passwords with as many digits as possible, include letters and symbols as well as numbers. Use different passwords for different websites as often as possible. You can use a password managing app to keep track of these if you can't remember them, but make sure to keep the app secure!

If the company you're dealing with allows two factor authentication, definitely give that a shot. Two factor authorization usually requires your password and an additional password that is either texted to your phone or a randomly generated number on a special token the company provides you with, which must be entered within a certain amount of time. It's a great safety feature.

You're done for the week! Next week will be more stereotypical personal finance and less paranoid computer nerd, I promise.

Week Three

The beginning of the real financial things is here! This week, we'll go over setting up automatic payments and contribution limits. This might even take less than three hours!

First things first, what are your fixed expenses? Rent/mortgage, internet, phone, and insurance should be costs that stay the same month after month. Are you able to automate those payments? Do you want to? We've discussed automation earlier and there are definite pros and cons. Depending on the type of person you are, automation could be amazing for you. You should make that decision this week. If you're interested in automating, there are a few options. You can have the vendor (the phone or internet company) charge your credit card directly (which is automated), and then have that same credit card automatically paid off as well. Or, you could have the payments come out of your bank account if you set up the vendors as bills in your online banking account. Some people really care about credit card rewards and will be willing to go that extra step. That's fine, this is a personal choice. But make sure you make a definitive choice and set up your accounts accordingly.

The second thing I'm going to ask you to do this week is to figure out your personal contribution limits for your RRSP and TFSA. The TFSA limit is quite easy to figure out. Were you 18 or older in 2009? If so your limit in 2017 is $52,000. You have to take off some amounts if you were younger. The limits from 2009-2012 were $5,000, 2013 and 2014 were $5,500, 2015 was $10,000, and after that it's gone back down to $5,500. Reduce as necessary depending on when you turned 18.

Your RRSP limit is a bit more complicated and can be figured out a few different ways. The easiest way is to take a look at your latest Notice of Assessment (NOA), a letter you get from the CRA after filing your taxes. It should have a total RRSP contribution room remaining on it. If you can't find that letter, you can also call the CRA or create an account on their website. The online account will take some time since they insist on mailing you the password. If you're okay with a quick estimate until you get your next NOA, simply add up all the income you've earned in your life, and multiply by 18%. This works if you didn't make more than $130,000 in any one year because of the upper limit on contributions per year. Subtract any contributions you've made in the past and you get your current limit.

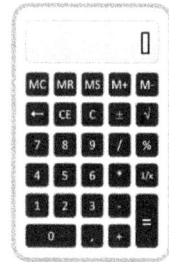

Write your contribution limits down somewhere and keep them for Week Five.

Week Four

Still saving your receipts? Good, keep doing that. We won't use them this week, but I just wanted to remind you to continue collecting them. A strong spending history is key to a good budget.

This week, we'll be setting financial goals. It'll be a deep and introspective three hours, so get comfy.

What do you want money for? It's a simple question, but it rarely has a simple answer. For a simple place to start, rank the following items in order of importance:

- Owning a home
- Owning a vehicle
- Fully funded retirement
- Great vacations every year
- Ability to buy whatever I want, whenever

Add items as you think of them. Do this honestly, you'd only be fooling yourself if you said you cared about retirement but really you just want to party lavishly every Saturday. That being said, retirement should be somewhere in the middle unless you're interested in early retirement (a teaser on that in the next section). Take your time and think deeply, what do you want to accomplish in the next 5, 10, and 15 years? These thoughts should include your working and personal life as well. Financial goals are only there to support your personal and work goals. If you want a family and a nice home for them, saving for a down payment allows you to do that. Financial goals are not the end goals, they support the real goals. What do you want?

Write out your 5, 10, and 15 year personal and work goals out on a piece of paper. What financial things do you need to do or have to make them happen?

If in 5 years you want to be promoted a few times and get a higher salary, would moving closer to work help out with that? Will it be more expensive than your current housing situation? Or maybe you'll want to buy a car at some

point in the future. If you want a family in 10 years, how much do you think you'll spend on a wedding and a home if you want to buy it? How many kids do you want to have and how much would providing for each one cost? How much money would you like to spend in retirement? You may not need to save for some of these goals now, but just being aware that you'll need to focus your money on things other than retirement will be good knowledge to have so you can allocate when to save for what.

Life will change, but having some goals written down will help you plan out your current financial situation. Having the experience of thinking about these goals will also help you accommodate changing situations into these plans when they arise.

Week Five

It's budget time! This week, you'll create a budget of what your actual spending looks like, without any help from receipts or online accounts. You'll be guessing.

The point in this exercise is to show you how people's views on where and what they spend money on differ from reality. Many people spend money without really paying attention and thinking about their spending, like a morning coffee or a pack of gum. So much so that they forget they made these purchases. The money just disappeared. You might be the one special snowflake that gets it right on, but let's see.

Start with your income, what do you bring home after payroll deductions every month? If you're self-employed you will need to make your own deductions, so definitely keep those in mind. Most people would probably only know this number to the nearest fifty or a hundred dollars. That's fine.

Next, deduct fixed expenses, these should be the easiest things to estimate since they don't generally change. Rent or mortgage payments, insurance payments (home or renter's), lease/car loan payments and insurance if you have a car, and phone and internet costs. That's a huge chunk of income gone, moving on.

Now we're getting into the more subjective stuff: food, entertainment, grooming, and miscellaneous. You may have more line items here, depending on how you spend your money. Some people might have a line item for clothing purchases, some might have a line item for alcohol, and some people have pets. If you spend more than 5% of your income on it, I think it deserves a separate line item. How much do you think you spend per month on each line? It may be helpful to think of some items on the annual level and then divide by 12, like pet expenses.

Have you saved any imaginary money? If you have that's great. If you were struggling to get within your income then we're finding an issue. This exercise should not have taken longer than 30-45 minutes. The rest of the time should be used to compare the pretend budget to your actual spending.

We're now going to use those saved receipts, credit history, and debit history. They will help you compare your estimate to actual spending. Add up and classify all of your spending for as many months as you have information for, up to four months. This will take up the remaining time this week. Compare your actual spending to the budget you created. This comparison is for knowledge and shock factor only. We won't be making any decisions on budgets this week.

How good were your estimates? Especially in the last category of budget items, most people will be wildly off from where they thought they would be. This is to be expected and goes to show that most people don't know where their money goes.

Homework for this week: I'd like you to read the budgeting methods and aides sections again. Be prepared to choose which one you want to use.

Week Six

You'll be doing more thinking this week.

What I want you to do this week is think about your relationship with money. What are your financial strengths and weaknesses? What are your personal (and maybe even religious) beliefs about money? What's your attitude towards money? How does your family address money? We're not trying to put blame on anyone, just trying to get an understanding of where you come from when it comes to dealing with money. Change is not easy, but it'll be easier if you know what could be holding you back.

These are key questions whose answers will guide you to the best way for you personally to accomplish your financial goals. Write everything that comes to mind down.

Examples of financial strengths would be:

- Always paying bills on time
- Living within your means without debt (unless education or housing)
- Having an understanding of investing, no matter how simple
- Having savings

Examples of some financial weaknesses would be:

- Being late on bills often
- Using credit cards to buy something that you know you can't pay for immediately
- Avoiding learning about investing because it scares you

Feel free to make a game out of it and see which side you score higher on, weaknesses or strengths. If it's weaknesses, don't worry, this book was made for you.

Is money good or evil in your mind? Do you view having money as a separator, dividing people into classes? Do you equate being poor with being pious? Nothing I can say about saving money will change the way you already treat money if you internalize it as an unattractive thing to have. I choose to view money as a tool, not good or evil. It's the person who wields it that gets to decide what it will do. If you want to use your money to give to a charity or help out your family, that's great. If you choose to buy food you never eat and throw out later, that's a different story.

What were your family's attitudes towards money? Were there arguments about money, or were there no issues that you knew of? Were you given an allowance and did anybody sit you down as a kid to talk about money? Was it openly discussed or kept secret from the children? Did your household experience financial hardship? Was there tension caused by monetary problems? All these factors will shape how you view spending and saving money in adulthood. What about your peers growing up? Were you the poor kid or the rich kid amongst friends in school? How did they treat you as a result?

What about your current attitude towards money? Do you appreciate the money you get from work, or treat it more along the lines of 'easy come easy go'? Are you more short term or long term oriented when it comes to life and/or money? Why?

How early did you start working? Try to remember what you did with the money you got in high school and maybe even your paper route in middle school. Why do you think you spent it the way you did?

Everyone learns a certain way when it comes to money. The best thing you can do for yourself is identify your own biases and think about how they will impact your ability to reach the financial goals you set in Week Four. Create action items for yourself on anything you want to overcome or change.

Week Seven

How does your actual spending align with your financial goals? This week, you'll choose a budgeting method or aide as well as doing a first draft of a budget that will be more in line with your goals. Are you saving enough for retirement? For that home you wanted to buy in ten years?

Week Five's homework was to take a read of the budgeting methods and aides in Part Two. Did you do that? If not, do it now.

What budgeting method appeals to you? Consider your personality traits and ingrained attitude towards money. Using a digital budgeting method like Mint is only as good as your ability to stay on top of spending and making sure to check the app or site often to see if you're on track with your goals and budget categories, and then change your behaviour if you're not.

Now that you've chosen a budgeting method, you need to set up your budget. If you're using an online application to help you, you'll need to link it up with all your accounts. Do that this week. If you're using a DIY approach and creating a budget in Excel, there is a template you can use on my website[54]. You can also make your own if you know what you want it to look like.

Now for the first reduction. How much do you need to save each month to get to your financial goals? Keep this number in the back of your head. You probably won't reach it at this level since this is the first cut to expenses. Look at the budget of expenses from Week Five, the one where you summarized your actual expenses month over month. Of this list of expenses, what purchases bring you the most joy? Do you love your apartment or love eating out with friends? Fantastic, I won't take that away from you. Make a list of your expenses in order from most happiness producing to least. If you have a lot of small, but similar expenses like morning coffee you can lump them together. Do not lump different restaurants together though. These are a prime elimination spot since you probably like one restaurant a lot more than another. If one expense cannot be separated from another, like rent and renter's insurance, they should share a line item on the list.

You've probably created a massive list of expenses. Start crossing out the ones you can sacrifice for your financial goals. Go only as far as 15% of current spending, we don't want to get over ambitious. If you currently spend $2,500 a month on living life, only cross out items worth $375 at most. We'll reassess in a few weeks after you've lived with this budget for a month or so. Hold yourself to this new budget for the next month and see how you do.

Week Eight

This week's exercise will be a bit annoying, you've been warned. You're going to look at your fixed expenses and try to reduce them. You might have to yell at your phone company or be on hold for a while, sorry.

Let's get started! Take all the bills out of the Utilities tab in your folder, or open the Utilities folder in your online organization system. These items should include: rent or mortgage payments, renters or home insurance, utility bills (electricity and water), phone, internet, public transportation passes, and car payments and insurance if you have them. Lay them out on the table. What can you painlessly reduce?

Your rent or mortgage payment is probably the biggest part of your spending every month, but we'll start with home/renter's insurance. Take a look online at the competing companies and see if their rates are lower than what you're getting. Now, you should call or email your insurance provider to see if they can get you a better deal than the one you have. Mention your good payment history and low risk as a client as well as the competing offers. Hopefully you get a few bucks off. Next comes the rent or mortgage payment. With rent, the only way to reduce it is to move somewhere else after your lease has expired. Would you be willing to do that to reduce costs? I'll leave that up to you, but make sure you account for moving costs too. Now a mortgage payment is something that can be reduced without changing homes. Has the interest rate in the marketplace gotten lower since you took out your mortgage? Can you refinance at a rate that's at least 1% lower? If this looks like a possibility, it might be worthwhile to look at refinancing at the lower rate to pay less interest. If you think you can accommodate increased mortgage payments, you can also look at shortening your loan timeline in order to pay less interest over time.

Utilities bills are fairly static without a change in behaviour. Are you willing to use less water in your life or watch the clock when you use electricity, in order to save a few dollars each month? Then go right ahead and make a plan to do that. You should, however, assess if you've been using these resources in a mindless way in the past; just being mindful of the limited nature of freshwater and energy generation could lower your use. As far as return on investment on time and effort I would put this item quite low on the list, you can only use so little.

Phone and Internet! This is where your main savings could be. Are you paying more than $100 per month on your phone? You can absolutely do better. There are many cheaper phone companies out there now with great service. Also check your data usage over the last few months, did you really need the full data amount that's included in your plan? Can you use WiFi at work and at home to reduce the data you use through the phone? Take a look at the plans offered by the phone companies that are competing with yours; you might be surprised how much lower you can go without losing service quality. Do make sure you check for contract breaking fees with your current carrier to see if switching is still worth it. Take a week or so to mull over this change and research potential companies' reviews. Do the same analysis with your internet provider. The alternatives are there, you just need to look for them. You may also be able to get better deals with your current provider by giving their retention phone line a call and pretending to leave or simply asking if they can do better. If you do call, remember to be assertive but polite.

Next up are transportation expenses. We'll start with car payments and insurance. For insurance, go over the same process as with the home or renter's insurance. With car payments, are you leasing or paying the loan on a car? Do you really need to own this exact car? Does it give you joy, or would a cheaper car suffice for your needs? Cars are a notoriously expensive asset that only decreases in value (unless we're talking vintage cars or very well-maintained used cars). Because of this, it's very expensive to drive a nice new car. If you have more car than you really need, whether in size or brand name, consider reducing the expense by selling the current vehicle and getting another. You could also consider making the switch to public transit or bicycling if your area supports those alternatives, they're much cheaper! Downsizing cars is not for everyone. If your car brings you ridiculous amounts of joy, that's absolutely fine.

That's it for this week!

Week Nine

This week is about taking care of debt, raising your credit score, and simplifying your credit situation. If you don't have debt you'll have a lighter assignment this week, enjoy it!

Pull out the credit score or report you received in Week Two. If you have a score, how happy are you with this score? Do you have large debt coming up that you need a good score for? If you don't, simply work on getting the good habits that are necessary for a good credit score: paying bills in full on time, not opening too many cards at once (or at all), and keeping a low utilization rate. If you're looking at a big purchase in the next few years, you might want to go deeper into the report and note how you could improve your score. Are there small outstanding balances you didn't know about? You should also be careful of paying off large or old loans right before the big purchase since your score will drop with the elimination of the debt. It's somewhat counterintuitive, but that's how it is.

Next, we'll look at how many debts you have outstanding. Do you have many credit cards that you don't use? How many store specific credit cards do you have? Do these cards serve a purpose in your life, or did you get them just because? A simplified credit card system could help you with keeping on top of your bills. If you don't have immediate refinancing or new debt on the horizon, pay off and close as many cards as you feel is appropriate. Your credit score will recover in a year or less with good debt behaviour.

Next comes current debt. What type of debts do you have? Student, mortgage, or credit card debt? Is any of it open to refinancing at a lower rate than the one you currently have? Can you safely do a balance transfer type of loan? What type of fees would those actions incur and would it be worth it? Call around and inspect all of your documentation to make sure you know about any prepayment and overpayment terms. Some lenders will not accept more than the monthly amount because they want to keep earning that interest.

Now that you have an idea of the loans that you have against you, prioritize them using either the snowball or avalanche technique, whichever you feel works with your personality. These techniques are discussed in the personal finance section if you forgot about them. Once you have the debts prioritized, set up a timeline to being debt free. How long will it take at your current, slightly reduced, budget to reach $0 net worth? Mark each debt's payoff time in the timeline and create a competition with yourself to see if you can strike those debts away at the allotted times.

On top of this, what changes are you willing to make in order to pay off the debts faster? Remember that if your debts are low interest, you may be better off investing the money instead of paying off the debt, so that option should also be considered.

Week Ten

Wow, Week Ten! Almost halfway through this journey, how does it feel so far? Are you getting the hang of paying your bills on time, being mindful of spending, and incorporating your long term goals into the mix?

This week, we'll create a routine to further solidify good financial behaviour into habit. When to update your budget, when to assess it, and when to calculate your net worth.

When you're just starting the process of getting your financial life in order, I would recommend the following weekly routine:

- Update your budget with spending for the week
- If using digital budget aides that are connected to your bank accounts, check that all of your spending has been categorized properly
- Assess how you did so far in the month against your spending reduction plans and debt reduction plans
- File any new money-related paperwork in the filing system
- Pay off credit cards if not using automatic payments
- If you have investments, assess how much you can put into investing

I recommend doing these activities on a weekly basis so that you get used to thinking about money in your daily life, it shouldn't take longer than an hour a week. The goal isn't to stress you out about your debt or your lack of discipline with money. It's about reminding you of your goals and their importance, despite their potentially very long timeline. Once you've done this for a few months you can move to twice a month, and then finally to once a month after six months or so. Once a month is the minimum frequency I would suggest, since forgetfulness starts to kick in around then and your records won't be as good.

Once you're in the once a month club, you can add the following to your money routine:

- Net worth update
- Buying investments according to the investing allocation you'll create in Week Sixteen
- Updating financial goals if they've changed

Week Eleven

Time to go back to your budget again! Are you starting to think about each purchase and whether it makes you happy?

This week, we'll take a look at the adjusted budget you created in Week Seven and compare your actual spending over the last month to what you predicted.

How did you do? Were there some items that you just couldn't go lower on, and some that you happily forgot how much you used to spend on? If this is the case, this means you have a clear distinction between spending that makes you happy and spending that's just spending. This is good, because it'll allow you to see which portions of the budget can be reduced further and which ones should not be. Go line by line comparing actual spending to budgeted spending, and explore why you may have failed to reach some reduction goals, or if you reduced beyond what you had budgeted on some line items.

Repeat the same exercise from Week Seven: Make a list of your expenses in order from most happiness producing to least. Remember to lump small expenses of the same type together and separate expenses that might be similar but provide you different levels of happiness. Take the list and remove 5-15% of the least-loved expenses again. You can also remove more if you've actually spent less than predicted last month and think you can go even further. But don't push yourself too hard; make sure to take things slow and steady. There's no point in rushing if you're going to angrily quit because you made the budget too restrictive.

It's at this point that I also want you to take a long hard look at what you've been buying at the grocery store. Remember all those grocery store receipts I've asked you to save since Week One? Get them all out now and go through them line by line. Are you seeing any trends towards buying small items that don't increase your happiness? The common ones would be gum, magazines, chocolate, or soft drinks that you pick up in the checkout aisle. If you have this habit and agree that it doesn't make you happy, you can include this in your cost cutting wish list for the month. You now have a new budget to try and stick to for the next month, let's see how well you do. This may or may not be the final budget, depending on your goals.

Speaking of goals, by now you should be on your way to an emergency fund if you decided you needed one. Is the fund fully financed to the level you've decided you needed? Do you have a separate bank account for it, or is it lumped into other savings? How are you doing on your debt repayment timeline or financial goals? Take the time this week to assess whether your new budget will be enough to reach those goals, or if you need to cut back even further.

Week Twelve

This week, we'll think long and hard about your job and how you feel about it. If you don't have a job or some means of income because you're a student or unemployed, you can skip this week's activity.

Let's look at your current role first. Are you happy where you are? Are your responsibilities in line with your skills and experience level? How long do you plan to stay at this role? Do you think the pay is reasonable? Is the role a permanent position, or do you foresee it being eliminated for whatever reason? Does your boss think you're doing a good job and do you have a good relationship with him or her? This analysis is not necessarily financial first and foremost, but it's useful to think about in the grand scheme of things. It also helps refine the size of your emergency fund.

Now let's talk about the company that you work for. Will it still be around in five years? What about 20? Is there room for growth for you and your skills within this organization? Have you heard any news about impending changes to management or the business structure? Do you want to move somewhere else?

Use these thoughts to help tweak your emergency fund requirements. If you intend on moving to a new company, how long do you realistically think you would be unemployed for? Is there a lot of demand for your skills in your industry? If your company or position is not rock solid, how long would it take you to find a new job? What kind of severance can you expect in that event? Take all of these factors into account when deciding the size of your emergency fund.

On a less depressing note, how awesome are your perks? Go through your offer letter or Human Resources website to find out what the company offers. Many will offer some sort of retirement planning help, maybe an RRSP match. If you haven't taken advantage of this already, get that paperwork in. Additionally, many employers offer perks regarding employee pricing for certain services that you could have missed when looking for ways to cut spending. Many of these are coupons for restaurants, reduced rate phone plans, fitness plans, and other reduced rate entertainment. You can use these discounts to reduce your spending further if you are paying more than you have to for some services.

Week Thirteen

It's time to see what kind of investor you are. This week, we'll go through assessing your risk profile, investment style, and doing a rough portfolio allocation.

How do you feel about investing? Do you think that you can handle risk, or are you terrified of losing even a cent in the stock market? This week, you should take the time to take the short quiz in Part Three of this book and one or more of the longer quizzes available in many places online. These quizzes will help you determine how risk averse you are and what type of investments would be best for you. They will also point you towards what your investment mindset likely is. Feel free to take some time to reread that section and the investment definitions section to refresh your memory on what types of investments are available to you.

Next you should think about your style of investing. Will you be excited about researching new investments and actively moving them around often to get the best deal around? Or are you more likely to want a more hands off approach for steady growth without too much involvement? Active investors are usually people who live and breathe investing, it excites them and they're knowledgeable about the terms and options. You'd know if this was you. Passive investors are generally not interested in the nitty gritty details of investing and just want to make a good return with the minimum amount of work possible. Decide what type of style would fit best with your lifestyle and knowledge of investing.

Now that you know your risk profile and investing style, you can come up with a basic asset allocation for yourself. How much of each type of investment do you think you should have? This mostly hinges on your risk profile and ability to handle ups and downs in the value of investments. Take a look at the investment examples in Part Three for ideas.

Week Fourteen

This week's activity is pretty relaxed, especially compared to last week's.

We'll be taking a look at all the accounts you have with various financial institutions. Look over your financial information folder and all the cards you have, credit and debit. Why do you have these particular accounts with these particular institutions? When you first opened the accounts, was it because you did a lot of research on each institution and the perks of each account, or just because you needed a bank account? Many people use a particular bank because their parents do, or because it was the first one they thought of, not because of any particular perks it gave them. I want you to take some time and research each account you have to see if you're happy with the services they offer and are getting the best deal. Look at what the competition offers and see if your decision still makes sense. Judge the bank based on customer service, account fees, whether they have easy to use online banking, if the rewards on the cards are good enough, and whatever else you value.

I would like to caution you against hopping around trying to find the best interest rate on savings accounts though. This wastes a lot of energy for a very small reward. Interest rates change so often that you'll be moving accounts every half a year or so, it's just not worth it. Find a bank that does well on the features above and stay the course.

But what accounts do you need? A chequing and savings account that should be with the same institution. These will facilitate everyday expenses and savings for items like vacations. I would also like you to put your emergency fund in a separate bank account, potentially in another institution. You need to be able to separate that account from your regular financial stuff since it's not for everyday use. The account should still be accessible and easy to take money out of in the case of an emergency, but you shouldn't have to look at it every day and see it as free money that's just sitting there waiting to be spent. We'll talk about investing accounts in a few weeks, stay tuned.

Week Fifteen
Time to go back to your budget again! Was this month even easier than the last one, or did you struggle to cut down even further? Are you continuing to be mindful of the correlation between spending and your happiness levels with each purchase?

This week, we'll take a look at the adjusted budget you created in Week Eleven and compare actual spending over the last month to what you predicted. And then compare it again to the old budget from Week Seven to show your progress.

How did you do? Was there more pain in spending less this time than the last? If this is the case, this means you're close to going too far with cutting down your expenses. Once you start feeling deprived there's no benefit from cutting further. That's not to say that you should feign deprivation to have a fatter budget, of course. By deprived, I mean you are legitimately unhappy, not just merely uncomfortable, with your spending. At the end of the day, the person who will lose is you when your retirement and other financial goals aren't met because you decided that a certain expense that could have been easily reduced and wasn't providing you with happiness was too important to give up. In the same manner as Week Eleven, go line by line comparing actual spending to your budgeted spending and explore why you may have failed to reach some reduction goals, or reduced even more than you had budgeted on some line items.

Repeat the same exercise from Week Eleven: Make a list of your expenses in order from most happiness producing to least. Take the list and remove 5-15% of your least loved expenses again. You can also remove more if you've actually spent less than you predicted last month and think you can go even further. Again, don't push yourself too hard. Reduce as much as you think is feasible for you to stop spending on within the month.

You should also assess your progress on your debt reduction and other financial goals. How is the emergency fund looking? Your savings account? Are you ready to think more about investing?

Week Sixteen

This will be another week all about investing, I know you're super excited!

In Week Thirteen you decided what type of investor you're going to be. This week, we'll take that further by having you choose a brokerage and refine your asset allocation.

All four of the types of brokerages we discussed in Part Three of the book will work with a passive investing style. Active investors will be more interested in the Independent Brokerage or Bank Hosted Brokerage types since they allow more freedom to invest however you like. Review the advantages and disadvantages of each broker type to make sure you fully understand what you're getting into. Changing your brokerages is easy when you have very little money, but once you have a sizeable nest egg, it'll be much harder to move stuff around. Try to make the right decision the first time.

Once you've decided which brokerage type you want to go with, do some research on the companies and options within that brokerage type. Several different companies might be offering the same services in your area. Try not to put too much faith in blog posts reviewing the services, since they are most likely paid reviews. For the most unbiased advice check forums and message boards within the investing community.

Once you've decided which specific company will be your brokerage, open an investing account! What type of account you open is really up to you. With most brokerages, you have the option of investing your money through an RRSP, a TFSA, or a taxable account. You should decide which account is best for you using the guidance on choosing between a TFSA and RRSP in Part Four of the book. The taxable account is for those who already have the maximum amounts invested through the tax advantaged types of accounts.

Opening the account will usually take a few days, since it requires identification to be verified and the transaction of moving your money to the brokerage to clear with your bank. You can set it in motion this week, but it likely won't be finished till we meet again in Week Seventeen. That's okay, since we won't be investing till Week Eighteen. You should initially only put in the minimum amount that the account requires to be opened, likely $1. Since you're not going to be investing for at least two weeks I don't want you to feel like you're losing out on potential gains.

Once you've set the brokerage account opening in motion, take a look at your asset allocation again. Do you still agree with it? Play around with fake calculations and simulations of what could have happened to your chosen allocation at times like the recession in 2008 and see how these calculations make you feel. Do you think you could stomach those types of swings?

You can always tweak your allocation once you actually start investing, but I just want you to understand how you would react in extreme circumstances given your current allocation.

Week Seventeen

It's time to think about taxes, will you do your own? Or are you going to hire a professional to do them for you? This week, we're going to look at making that decision and what kind of documentation you're going to have to keep in your Taxes folder until tax time.

When it comes to filing taxes, whether you decide to tackle it yourself or have a professional file them for you boils down to three things. Your skills and knowledge regarding tax filing and how complicated the return would be. When your income only comes from one employer and investment trading is kept to a minimum, even relatively non-knowledgeable people can prepare their own taxes. Check out Part Four for a walkthrough of some common income types and deduction. If you own some rental properties and a business on top of employment income and are an active investor you might want to contact a professional. This decision should also be made while considering costs since non-complex tax returns are not cheap.

Regardless of your decision about who will file your taxes for you, you still have to collect all the documentation. The documentation that you'll need to provide for tax filing is:
- T4 schedules provided by your employer
- T5 schedules provided by your brokerages
- RRSP contribution slips provided by your retirement account holding companies (potentially also your brokerage)
- Receipts for all deductible expenses

- Credit card statements for deductible expenses without receipts
- Information regarding the sale and costing of any investments you sold in the year
- If you have a rental property, support for income and deductions
- If you have a business, support for income and deductions

Keep all this information in a safe place, preferably in the Taxes folder in your organization system, until you file the taxes based on this information. After filing, you should save the information in case of an audit or reassessment. Keep the information around as long as required by your province.

Week Eighteen

Another investment focused week! This week you'll put actual money into your brokerage account and put your asset allocation to good use by researching and picking investments.

The first thing to decide is how much money you want to be investing right now. This depends on how much you have saved up outside of your emergency fund, and whether you have those savings allocated to something more important than investing, like a down payment. This is dependent entirely on your financial goals. Whatever amount you have sitting there that's not spoken for, dump it all into an investment account, at once. You read that right. Remember what we discussed earlier in Part Three about trying to time investments, be rational.

If your brokerage is a robo advisor or a personal financial advisor, your work stops here for the week. You would've set investing preferences with either brokerage when you opened the account and they'd invest your money accordingly. They'll take their fee, of course, but you'll never research investments.

If you chose the other brokerage types, you'll also do some research on your chosen investment types. Take out your asset allocation from the previous weeks and make sure you're still happy with what it looks like. Have you considered all investment types, or just stocks and bonds when making this allocation?

Make sure you consider whether any or all of the ones outlined in Part Three are right for your portfolio. This exercise will allow you to decide which asset types you should have in your portfolio and how much of each. When assessing which ones are right for you, consider not only your risk portfolio, but also the diversification, currency fluctuations, management expense ratios, and transaction fees that are associated with them.

Once you have decided on asset types, you can start looking for the right securities to invest in. A couple of quick Google searches for "the best ETF/REIT/mutual fund/bond index for..." will get you started. If you want to trade individual stocks, you're going to have to come up with an investing checklist or mandate to make sure you stick to your guns. I would not recommend individual stocks to beginners. Index funds (either in ETF or mutual fund form) are a great start for a novice investor. They literally just follow the market. It can't get easier than that, and they're cheap. REITs are also a good place to start for those who love real estate. Once you've done all the research and have decided on which assets you want to hold, it's time to decide where you want to hold them.

Think back to the investing portion of this book, were taxes a big deal when it comes to choosing investments? No, but they should be considered when deciding where to hold your investments. Go back to read over the taxation of investment gains part in order to decide how best to spread out your chosen allocation of investments across the tax advantaged and taxable accounts.

Okay, now you know what you're buying and where. Do it up! Buy up all the securities you've chosen in the right proportions. If you can't pull the trigger quite yet, you can wait till next week and do it then. But don't wait any longer or you'll get a case of analysis paralysis and that just ruins things.

Week Nineteen

So, you're either already invested or are about to invest. Go ahead and do that. This week will be

about creating an investing schedule and rules around investing to make things easier for yourself.

To create an investing schedule, you'll have to consult your budget. How much money do you have left over every month or every two weeks (depending on how you do your budgeting) that is not ear marked to pay down debt or save for an emergency fund or other specialized reason? This is the money you can use to invest. Create a goal or a rule to invest this amount of money each time it's available to you. You can set this as an automated bill in your bank account if you're not skittish about those. Alternatively, you can also set a rule for yourself that once you've accumulated a certain amount of savings, you'll dump in into investment accounts. A common and manageable amount would be $1,000.

Now you'll do more or less the same with money that's already in your investing accounts. Set a rule for yourself that once the cash balance gets above a certain point, probably that same $1,000, that you'll convert it into actual investments.

Creating these rules for yourself will create a situation where you don't second-guess decisions about investing. It's a very emotional process and it's best to remove as much emotion as possible from your invested money. It's there to serve a purpose, let it do that without being worried about it all the time. Set it, forget it, profit.

You should keep an eye on that asset allocation of yours and the percentages of each type of asset in it, though. Over time, your investments will change in value and will no longer be aligned in the same way as when you bought them. If you invest regularly, you can easily re-align them with new purchases of investments. If you don't invest regularly, you should set a time to look over your investments and re-balance them back to your preferred allocation. If you're a passive investor, every quarter is a good routine. You should decrease frequency of your rebalancing over time.

Week Twenty

It's budget time again! It's the last time we'll be looking at your budget during these six months. How did you do? Was this month even easier than the last one or did you cut down all you could in Week Fifteen?

This week, we'll take a look at the adjusted budget you created in Week Fifteen and compare actual spending over the last month to what you predicted. And then compare it again to old budgets from Weeks Seven and Eleven to show your progress.

Were you able to reduce your expenses again, or are you at the lowest possible budget? Like I said before, once you start feeling deprived there's no benefit from cutting expenses even further. In the same manner as Week Fifteen, go line by line comparing actual spending to budgeted spending and explore why you may have failed to reach some reduction goals or reduced even more than you had budgeted on some line items. This should be familiar by now.

Repeat the same exercise again: make a list of your expenses in order from most happiness producing to least. Take the list and see if you can remove 5-15% of the least loved expenses again. Reduce as much as you think is feasible for you to stop spending on within the month. If you don't think you can reduce anything further, that's okay too. We've already gone through so many reductions that at this point you should be getting to the point where you've created a comfortable budget that will help you reach your financial goals without being too restrictive and depriving you of happiness.

You should also assess your progress on debt reduction and other financial goals. Are you ready to pile more money into your investing accounts yet ?

Week Twenty-One

This week, we'll focus on your buying behaviours. Are you prone to impulsively purchasing things regardless of whether you need them? Or do you generally pick the first or most well-known brand you see when you do need to buy something?

This week, you'll create a set of guidelines or checklist for yourself for buying large ticket items. If a purchase is worth more than $1,000, I'd say it deserves some thought and effort.

You can also institute a set of guidelines if you feel you have an issue with impulse purchases.

There's a list in Part Two of this book of some items that could go on a buying checklist, but you could also add your own.

And you're done! Do you feel like you've made some progress towards your financial goals in the last six-ish months? I really hope that following these steps has helped you get a hold of your life financially and given you the confidence to do so. Personal finance is pretty routine stuff once you get all the knowledge and habits down. Good luck!

6 Financial Independence

The holy grail of money stuff and a difficult thing to achieve. Financial independence (FI) is not needing to work to support yourself. It means having "f*** you" money to throw in an employer's face if they abuse you. If you are FI, you could just stop working altogether if you don't love your job. But for most people, being able to do these things is a daydream not to be taken seriously.

However, there is a growing subculture of individuals that are planning to retire in their 40s and 50s by saving a ridiculous amount of their annual salaries. I'm not saying this lifestyle is for everyone, but I wanted to take this short section a little further than normal finance books into slightly more philosophical territory.

What do you really want out of life? Do you spend the majority of your non-sleeping time doing that thing? Or do you spend it trying to fund your life full of convenience and boredom that stems from you working most of the day? Very few people can say they spend the majority of their day engaged in thoroughly satisfying activities.

I want to travel the world full time, am I doing that? No. I'm being an accountant every day. I'm sure you're in a similar position. But I don't plan on being an accountant my whole life, and this section of the book is about how to create financial independence.

You've been warned, this is advanced personal finance and is not for everyone. But read on if you're interested.

How to Get There

In order to have so much money that you don't need to work anymore, you need to get a huge chunk of cash. You sure won't get it in the lottery. So how do you get it?

The normal ways most people get money, but taken to the extreme. You could do it through earning a huge income (high salary or owning a company), or through saving a large part of a normal income.

Very few people will be able to supersize their income in a short period of time; most salaried positions don't work like that. And even when they do, those million-dollar salaries generally go to the top people in the company. If you can get to one of those positions, kudos. For the rest of us, there's the savings route.

The savings route is pretty simple: save enough every year to reach your financial independence number as soon as you want to reach it.

But how much is enough?

FI Number

Calculating the amount of money you need in order to peace out from the workforce is actually quite simple. But first, you must decide how much money you want to spend every year for the rest of your life. Easy, right?

If $40,000 is your number, multiply that by 25 and you get $1,000,000. That's how much money you need to have invested in order to take out $40,000 every year for 30 years.

If you can live on $20,000, that number drops to $500,000!

Why multiply by 25? And why only 30 years?

These numbers come from a research paper commonly called the Trinity study[55], where researchers tested how long a portfolio of a particular size would last a person if they took out a consistent amount every year, adjusted for inflation. The study relied on a pretty run of the mill mix of stocks and bonds which they ran through simulations using past stock market information. They came to the conclusion that a person can withdraw 4% of the starting portfolio's value each year, with increases for inflation, every year for 30 years without running out of money 95-98% of the time. We get the 25x spending factor by rearranging this withdrawal formula.

To make the money last longer than 30 years or if you don't think the stock market will perform as well as it has in the past, you would need to reduce the percentage you take out every year, withdrawal rates of anywhere between 2-4% are popular.

To calculate how long it would take you to get to this number, you need to first calculate something called savings rate.

$$\text{Savings rate} = (\text{Savings / After tax pay}) \times 100$$

If I make $50,000 after taxes and spend $25,000, my savings is $25,000 and therefore my savings rate is 50%. With a rate like that, I can expect to get to my FI number in 17 years. The higher the savings rate, the lower the number of years to get there.

There's a cool website that will calculate how many years you have left till you reach your number which you can play with[56].

Your FI number can be pretty daunting. To work yourself up to it, you might first get to something called a coasting number and reassess whether you're interested in continuing.

Coasting Number

A coasting number, or Barista FI as it referred to in the community, is the amount of money that will grow to your desired FI number by itself given the time to normal retirement age. So, if you were the first individual who needed $40,000 per year to live on and were looking to hit Barista FI by 30 years of age, you would have 35 years for compounding to do its magic. So what's the number that gets you to a million in 35 years? Around $185,000. That's less than 20% of your independence number! It's like a down payment for your independence.

The idea with Barista FI is that once you get there you only have to earn enough to support yourself without adding to the financial independence fund. You're supposed to let the money grow while you take care of your own expenses. But you can't take anything out of it, either. It's a nice halfway point between complete financial independence and a relaxed approach to work.

It allows you to take a break and leave the workforce for a bit if you like and have enough to support yourself for that time period.

That's pretty much it! A very basic intro to get you started without boring you too much.

Conclusion

That's a wrap!

Personal finance is something we're not really taught nowadays but are expected to know when we get out there into the adult world. As a result, many people stumble. They rack up debt, spend thoughtlessly, and end up in a situation where they're unhappy and broke. This book aims to mitigate the effects of these stumbles and provide information to help you build a strong financial future. You can do it!

Thanks for reading, I hope this book has helped you set financial goals for yourself and provided enough support for you to start working towards them.

I'm available at HTA.author@gmail.com if you have questions. I'd love to hear your story if the book has helped you!

For free content and additional information please visit my website at www.HTAbook.com

References

[1] Botvinnik, Victoria. "Free Content." *How to Adult - Money*. N.p., 2017. Web. 3 Apr. 2017. <http://www.htabook.com/>.

[2] "Three-Quarters of Americans Worry About Having Enough Money to Retire." *Politics - Three-Quarters of Americans Worry About Having Enough Money to Retire*. The Harris Poll, 10 July 2014. Web. 3 Apr. 2017. <http://www.theharrispoll.com/politics/Three-Quarters_of_Americans_Worry_About_Having_Enough_Money_to_Retire.html>.

Part 1: Personal Finance

[3] Prelec, Drazen, and Duncan Simester. "Always Leave Home Without It: A Further Investigation of the Credit-Card Effect on Willingness to Pay." *Sloan School of Management, MIT - Marketing Letters* 12:1 (2001): 5-12. Kluwer Academic Publishers, 8 June 2000. Web. 3 Apr. 2017. <http://web.mit.edu/simester/Public/Papers/Alwaysleavehome.pdf>.

[4] *V Annual Income Statement - VISA Inc. CI A Annual Financials*. Marketwatch Inc., 20017. Web. 3 Apr. 2017. <http://www.marketwatch.com/investing/stock/v/financials>.

[5] Simon, Jeremy M. "FICO's 5 factors: The components of a credit score." *FICO's 5 factors: The components of a credit score.* CreditCards.com, 2017. Web. 3 Apr. 2017. <http://www.creditcards.com/credit-card-news/help/5-parts-components-fico-credit-score-6000.php>.

[6] *What To Do If You Find Errors in Your Credit Report?* Office of Consumer Affairs (OCA), 30 Nov. 2012. Web. 8 Apr. 2017. <https://www.ic.gc.ca/eic/site/oca-bc.nsf/eng/ca02181.html>.

[7] *Issue Brief: Credit Cards: Statistics and Facts*. Canadian Bankers Association, 18 Jan. 2017. Web. 8 Apr. 2017. <http://www.cba.ca/credit-cards>.

[8] Bostock, Mike, Shan Carter, and Archie Tse. "Is It Better to Rent or Buy?" *Is It Better to Rent or Buy? - The New York Times*. The New York Times, 2017. Web. 3 Apr. 2017. <https://www.nytimes.com/interactive/2014/upshot/buy-rent-calculator.html?_r=1>.

[9] *Mortgage Calculator*. Calculator.net, 2017. Web. 4 Apr. 2017. < http://www.calculator.net/mortgage-calculator.html>.

[10] 1.877.987.1420. CanadaMortgage.com, 2017. Web. 8 Apr. 2017. < http://www.canadamortgage.com/calculators/amortschedule.cgi>.

[11] *CMHC Insurance| Mortgage Insurance| CMHC Mortgage*

Calculator| CMHC Insurance Rates. RateHub, 2017. Web. 8 Apr. 2017. < https://www.ratehub.ca/cmhc-mortgage-insurance>.
[12] Ibid.
[13] *Canadian household debt-to-income ratio rises to record high 166.9%*. Bell Media, 14 Dec. 2016. Web. 8 Apr. 2017.
[14]*Snowball Vs Avalanche Calculator*. MagnifyMoney, 2017. Web. 3 Apr. 2017. <http://www.magnifymoney.com/calculator/snowball-avalanche-calculator/>.
[15] Botvinnik, Victoria. "Free Content." *How to Adult - Money*. N.p., 2017. Web. 3 Apr. 2017. <http://www.htabook.com/>.

Part 2: Budgets and Savings

[16]*Detached home price tops $1M in Markham, Richmond Hill*. YorkRegion.com, 7 Apr. 2015. Web. 8 Apr. 2017. <http://www.yorkregion.com/news-story/5544112-detached-home-price-tops-1m-in-markham-richmond-hill/>.
[17]*Future Value of an Annuity Calculator*. UltimateCalculators.com, 2010. Web. 4 Apr. 2017. < http://www.ultimatecalculators.com/future_value_annuity_calculator.html>.
[18] *Retirement Calculator - How much will I need to save for retirement?* CalcXML, 2017. Web. 4 Apr. 2017. <https://www.calcxml.com/calculators/retirement-calculator>.
[19] *Compound Interest Calculator*. Www.moneychimp.com, 2017. Web. 4 Apr. 2017. < http://www.moneychimp.com/calculator/compound_interest_calculator.htm>.
[20] Ibid.
[21]*Retirement savings calculator*. Sun Life Assurance Company of Canada, 2017. Web. 8 Apr. 2017. <https://www.sunlife.ca/ca/Learn and Plan/Tools and Calculators/Retirement savings calculator?vgnLocale=en_CA>.
[22] Botvinnik, Victoria. "Free Content." *How to Adult - Money*. N.p., 2017. Web. 3 Apr. 2017. <http://www.htabook.com/>.
[23] Ibid.
[24] Stefanac, Meg. Car *Depreciation: How Much Have You Lost?* Consumer Agent Portal, LLC, 14 Feb. 2014. Web. 4 Apr. 2017. <https://www.trustedchoice.com/insurance-articles/wheels-wings-motors/car-depreciation/>.
[25] *Ultimate Retirement Calculator*. Financial Mentor, 2017. Web. 4 Apr. 2017. <https://financialmentor.com/calculator/best-retirement-calculator>.
[26] Ibid

Part 3: Investing

[27] Verdi, Stefania Di. *How to win the lottery*. Rogers Media, 1 Feb. 2013. Web. 4 Apr. 2017. <http://www.moneysense.ca/spend/shopping/how-to-win-the-lottery-2/>

Blodget, Henry. *A Startup's Odds of Success Are Very Low*. Business Insider, 28 May 2013. Web. 4 Apr. 2017. <http://www.businessinsider.com/startup-odds-of-success-2013-5>.

[28] *Compound Interest Calculator*. Www.moneychimp.com, 2017. Web. 4 Apr. 2017. < http://www.moneychimp.com/calculator/compound_interest_calculator.htm>.

[29] *List of recessions in the United States*. Wikipedia, 2 Mar. 2017. Web. 4 Apr. 2017. <https://en.wikipedia.org/wiki/List_of_recessions_in_the_United_States>.

[30] Hall, Robert (October 21, 2003). "The NBER's Recession Dating Procedure". National Bureau of Economic Research. Retrieved April 4, 2017.

[31] *S&P/TSX Composite index (INDEXTSI:OSPTX) Historical Prices*. Google, 2017. Web. 5 Apr. 2017. <https://www.google.ca/finance/historical?q=INDEXTSI%3AOSPTX&ei=enL2WJCtC8eOjΛHUrIz4Dg>.

[32] Ibid.

[33] Linder, Douglas O. *Enron Stock Price Chart and Data*. UMKC School of Law, 2017. Web. 5 Apr. 2017. <http://www.famous-trials.com/images/ftrials/Enron/documents/enronstockchart.pdf>.

[34] *Apple Inc.(NASDAQ:AAPL) Historical Prices*. Google, 2017. Web. 5 Apr. 2017. <https://www.google.ca/finance/historical?q=NASDAQ:AAPL>.

[35] *S&P/Case-Shiller IL-Chicago Home Price Index*. Federal Reserve Bank of St. Louis, 2017. Web. 4 Apr. 2017. <https://fred.stlouisfed.org/series/CHXRSA>.

[36] On a $100,000 investment. *Mutual fund fee calculator*. Ontario Securities Commission, 2017. Web. 4 Apr. 2017. <http://www.getsmarteraboutmoney.ca/en/tools_and_calculators/calculators/Pages/mutual-fund-fee-calculator.aspx#.WG2eQFUrJxA>.

[37] Shufelt, Tim. *Actively managed funds vs. the index: once again, no contest*. The Globe and Mail, 13 Nov. 2014. Web. 4 Apr. 2017. <http://www.theglobeandmail.com/globe-investor/investment-ideas/actively-managed-funds-vs-the-index-once-again-no-contest/article21580578/>.

[38] Some weird ones here for your reading pleasure: Silverblatt, Rob.

The 10 Strangest Mutual Funds. U.S. News & World Report L.P., 2 Dec. 2009. Web. 4 Apr. 2017. <http://money.usnews.com/money/personal-finance/articles/2009/12/02/the-10-strangest-mutual-funds>.

[39] Barber, Brad M., and Terrance Odean. "All That Glitters: The Effect of Attention and News on the Buying Behavior of Individual and Institutional Investors." *The Review of Financial Studies* 21.2 (2008): n. pag. Web. 8 Apr. 2017.

[40]*Market-timing: A two-sided coin.* The Vanguard Group, Inc, Oct. 2010. Web. 8 Apr. 2017. <https://www.vanguardlearning.co.uk/sites/default/files/additional-resources/Market%20timing%20A%20two-sided%20coin.pdf>.

[41] *Determinants of Financial Market Spillovers: The Role of Portfolio Diversification, Trade, Home Bias, and Concentration* . International Monetary Fund, Oct. 2014. Web. 8 Apr. 2017. <https://www.imf.org/external/pubs/ft/wp/2014/wp14187.pdf>.

[42]*Vanguard Total World Stock ETF.* The Vanguard Group, Inc., 2017. Web. 4 Apr. 2017. <https://personal.vanguard.com/us/funds/snapshot?FundId=3141&FundIntExt=INT>.

Part 4: Taxes

[43] *Employee or Self-employed?*. Canada Revenue Agency, 2016. Web. 8 Apr. 2017. <http://www.cra-arc.gc.ca/E/pub/tg/rc4110/rc4110-16e.pdf>.

[44] *Employers' Guide: Taxable Benefits and Allowances.* Canada Revenue Agency, 2016. Web. 8 Apr. 2017. <http://www.cra-arc.gc.ca/E/pub/tg/t4130/t4130-16e.pdf>.

[45] *Capital Cost Allowance Rates, Capital Vs Expense.* TaxTips.ca, 27 Feb. 2017. Web. 8 Apr. 2017. <http://www.taxtips.ca/smallbusiness/ccarates.htm>.

[46] *Canadian income tax rates for individuals - current and previous years.* Canada Revenue Agency, 4 Jan. 2017. Web. 8 Apr. 2017. <http://www.cra-arc.gc.ca/tx/ndvdls/fq/txrts-eng.html>.

[47] *2016 and 2017 Tax Brackets and Tax Rates - Canada and Provinces/Territories.* Boat Harbour Investments Ltd, 14 Mar. 2017. Web. 4 Apr. 2017. <http://www.taxtips.ca/marginaltaxrates.htm>.

[48] Botvinnik, Victoria. "Free Content." *How to Adult - Money.* N.p., 2017. Web. 3 Apr. 2017. <http://www.htabook.com/>.

[49] *Certified software for the 2017 NETFILE program.* Canada Revenue Agency, 6 Apr. 2017. Web. 8 Apr. 2017. <http://www.cra-arc.gc.ca/esrvc-srvce/tx/ndvdls/netfile-impotnet/crtfdsftwr/menu-eng.html>.l

[50]*T4 Statement of Remuneration Paid (slip)*. Canada Revenue Agency, 18 Nov. 2014. Web. 8 Apr. 2017. <http://www.cra-arc.gc.ca/E/pbg/tf/t4/README.html>.

[51]*T5 Statement of Investment Income (slip)*. Canada Revenue Agency, 20 Nov. 2015. Web. 8 Apr. 2017. <http://www.cra-arc.gc.ca/E/pbg/tf/t5/README.html>.

Part 5: Six Months to Being Awesome With Money

[52]*Winnable Top View 13-Pocket Expandable Files*, Letter. Staples Canada Inc., 2017. Web. 8 Apr. 2017. <http://www.staples.ca/en/Winnable-Top-View-13-Pocket-Expandable-Files-Letter/product_658971_2-CA_1_20001>.

[53] *Pendaflex® 13 Pocket Cheque-Size File*. Staples Canada Inc., 2017. Web. 8 Apr. 2017. <http://www.staples.ca/en/Pendaflex-13-Pocket-Cheque-Size-File/product_618709_2-CA_1_20001>.

[54] Botvinnik, Victoria. "Free Content." *How to Adult - Money*. N.p., 2017. Web. 3 Apr. 2017. <http://www.htabook.com/>.

Part 6: Financial Independence

[55] Cooley, Philip L., Carl M. Hubbard, and Daniel T. Walz. "Sustainable Withdrawal Rates From Your Retirement Portfolio." Association for Financial Counseling and Planning Education, 1999. Web. 4 Apr. 2017. <http://afcpe.org/assets/pdf/vol1014.pdf>.

[56]*Early Retirement Calculator* . Networthify, 2017. Web. 4 Apr. 2017. <https://networthify.com/calculator/earlyretirement>.

Disclaimer

All information in this book is the property of Victoria Botvinnik or the entities cited and is protected by copyright and intellectual property laws. You may not reproduce, sell, or circulate the information found in this book without the express written consent of Victoria Botvinnik or the entities cited. All images unless otherwise noted are sourced from https://openclipart.org/ which allows commercial use of all it's images. Other images have been created by the author.

This book is presented solely for educational and entertainment purposes. The author and publisher are not offering it as legal, accounting, or investment advice. While best efforts have been used in preparing this book, the author makes no representations of any kind and assumes no liabilities of any kind with respect to the accuracy or completeness of the contents of this work. The author shall not be held liable or responsible to any person or entity with respect to any loss or incidental or consequential damages caused, or alleged to have been caused, directly or indirectly, by the information or programs contained herein. Every individual is different and the advice and strategies contained herein may not be suitable for your situation. You should seek the services of a competent professional before beginning any improvement program. The story and its characters and entities are fictional. Any likeness to actual persons, either living or dead, is strictly coincidental.

Although the author has made every effort to ensure that the information in this book was correct at press time, the author and publisher do not assume and hereby disclaim any liability to any party for any loss, damage, or disruption caused by errors or omissions, whether such errors or omissions result from negligence, accident, or any other cause.

All information in this book is the property of Victoria Botvinnik or the entities cited and is protected by copyright and intellectual property laws. You may not reproduce, sell, or circulate the information found in this book without the express written consent of Victoria Botvinnik or the entities cited.